'In our day...'

Perthshire is the adopted home to **MARGARET BENNETT** who was brought up on the islands of Skye, Lewis and Shetland in a family of tradition bearers, Gaelic on her mother's side and Scots on her father's. She is a folklorist, singer, writer, and part-time lecturer on the Scottish Music degree at the Royal Scottish Academy of Music and Drama. She 'wears her scholarship lightly', whether at home with her 'Ochtertyre Song Weekends', or at an international festival in North America. In handing on tradition, she inbues an infectious enthusiasm into her workshops, teaching songs in an enriched cultural context. A recipient of several previous awards, in 2010 she received an Honorary Doctor of Music from the RSAMD in recognition of her contribution to Scottish tradition. Author of several books, including *Scottish Customs from the Cradle to the Grave*, (2004) and her book with Doris (cited below), Margaret also sings on CD collaborations with her late son, Martyn—*Glen Lyon* is set in the heart of Perthshire. She is Patron of the Traditional Music

and Song Association and of 'Crofting Connections' (a Scottish Curriculum for Excellence project).

Born in Pitcairngreen, **DORIS ROUGVIE** is rooted in rural Perthshire where music and songs have always been a part of her daily life. A central figure on the Scottish folk scene, Doris is a popular guest at many festivals and folk clubs in Scotland and Ireland and has a pivotal role in Perthshire's Glenfarg Village Folk Club which attract international performers and audiences. Doris sings and tours with 'The Keekin Gless', (now on CD), a production devised by poet Carl MacDougall, featuring stories, songs, poems and music of Perthshire and with Dougie MacLean's 'Perthshire Amber Tour Bus'. She is well-known for hosting some of Scotland's most memorable 'singarounds', including the 'House of Song' at Glasgow's Celtic Connections Festival and her own Huntingtower fireside ceilidhs. Her recent CD, 'My Joy of You' reflects Doris's warmth and enthusiasm. A skilled craftswoman and artist, Doris has illustrated this book as well as a previous collaboration with Margaret, '*Then Another Thing'—Remembered in Perthshire* (1999). In 2009 she was awarded an Honorary Life Membership of the TMSA.

'In our day...'

REMINISCENCES AND SONGS FROM
RURAL PERTHSHIRE

Margaret Bennett

Margaret Bennett
Doris Rougvie & friends

A Grace Notes Scotland Collection

'In our day...'
Reminiscences and Songs from Rural Perthshire
First published 2010 by Grace Note Publications
in collaboration with Grace Notes Scotland
Grange of Locherlour, Ochtertyre, PH7 4JS, Scotland
books@gracenotereading.co.uk

ISBN 978-1-907676-02-4

British Library Cataloguing-in-Publications Data
A catalogue record for this book is available from the British Library

Typeset by Grace Note Publications C.I.C, Ochtertyre, Perthshire
Printed and Bound by Charlesworth Press, West Yorkshire

DEDICATED
to all who have contributed to this book
and to the folk whose Perthshire memories
continue to enrich our lives.

Contents

Foreword

Conversations and reminiscences of earlier times often begin 'in our day…' No matter which generation is speaking, personal memories not only reflect the teller's own lifetime, but may also include what parents, grandparents and even great-grandparents recalled. Without any reference to books, the remarkable span of oral tradition can range across two centuries or more. Often, however, such conversations quickly fade into the past, then, too late, we wish we had least made a note of details that seemed so clear and bright at the time. Yet, no matter how many recordings we make (or notes we write), there is always more waiting to be recorded—or lost forever.

It was a Caithness man, with high-ranking status in the British parliament, who first had the ambitious idea of recording for posterity current information on all aspects of Scottish society. Ideas are one thing; carrying them out, another. As it happened, however, Sir John Sinclair was also a lay member of the General Assembly of the Church of Scotland, and where better than the annual gathering in Edinburgh to hand out questionnaires to every parish minister, requesting a response. As might be expected, some were keener than others to write screeds about their local parish, but by 1791 he had enough to edit one volume of *The Statistical Account of Scotland.* Seven and a half years later, with contributions from over 900 ministers (and many reminders to reluctant writers) Sinclair completed the Herculean task he had set himself of editing and compiling *The Statistical Account* covering every parish in Scotland— twenty volumes in all.

Before long, the work was regarded as a 'model' that set

the standard across Europe, and it has been a main reference point for every enquiry about Scottish social history from the eighteenth century onwards. Two more have since appeared, *The New Statistical Account of Scotland (1844–45)*, thus, ever since, the first *Account* has been known as the *Old Statistical Account*, and the most recent, *The Third Statistical Account of Scotland*, undertaken and published between 1951 and 1992 (Volume 27, published in 1979, covers Perthshire). All three are regarded as primary sources for Scottish social, economic, ecclesiastical, cultural and linguistic history, and are often the starting place for historical researchers.

For oral historians and folklorists, the starting place is usually the spoken word, which may (or may not) be corroborated by a printed source. This miscellany from rural Perthshire has grown out of many conversations and also takes some of its inspiration from an earlier collection, *Remembered in Perthshire*, which Doris and I put together ten years ago. Our main source of information were residents in care homes —we began by singing a few songs, hoping some would join in, and unfailingly they not only sang with us but reminded us of a rich seam of local history and culture that continues to hold our interest. Most of the folk we recorded then are no longer with us, but their memories live on, as do their songs.

Reminiscences such as these, recording the way of life in rural Perthshire, are part of a long chain of memories stretching back to a time well before those written down by parish ministers in the 1790s. Over the years, local newspapers and community newsletters have added innumerable links to this chain. The oldest 'link' dates back to the time of John the Baptist, who, as everyone knows, subsisted on a diet of 'locusts and wild honey'. After a lifetime of imagining (or trying *not* to imagine) anyone having to eat some brittle, grass-hopper-like creature, even with a spoonful of honey, I can now put my mind at rest about the locusts. Read on—you may even wish to taste them!

Memories are not, however, the domain of the elderly alone, as readers will discover through these pages. The youngest contributors were born in the 21st century and are still in primary school. They deserve a special mention as they wrote to me after a 'story-telling visit' I made to their school, Errol Primary, this year. As one of them happened to give me the undeserved compliment of being 'really good at making up stories,' I immediately owned up and confessed that all my stories were told to me by other folk, such as my parents, grandparents, neighbours. "So if you ask *your* parents, grandparents, aunties, uncles, or anyone of any age you'll might be surprised what interesting memories they'll tell you…" With a great deal of enthusiasm (as well as encouragement from their teachers), off they set. Before long the postman delivered a fat envelope of 'Perthshire Memories' to me, some of which are printed here.

A huge thanks to all, young and old, who have allowed me to record their reminiscences and special thanks to Doris who shared visits with me as well as her enthusiasm, songs and her artistic skills. (She was also one of the team of transcribers who are mentioned later.)

In drawing together the stories for this book I hope that readers will not only enjoy glimpses of the past but will also be reminded of their own store of memories that deserve to be passed on. And, as Perthshire is celebrating 'Perth 800' in the year 2010, we have put together some of the many songs composed by Perthshire folk. Just as Perthshire's best-known song, 'The Rowan Tree', has given pleasure to every generation since it was first composed, may this collection be enjoyed for many years to come.

Margaret Bennett
Ochtertyre, Perthshire, 2010

1

The Auld Hoose...

Oh the auld hoose, the auld hoose, whit tho' the rooms were wee
Kind hearts were dwellin' there and bairnies fu' o glee...
> —Carolina Oliphant, (Lady Nairne),
> Gask House, Perthshire

Carolina Oliphant (1766—1845) was born in Gask House, her ancient family home overlooking the River Earn. She lived there till 1806, when she married William Murray Nairne, and later became Lady Nairne. Returning to Gask in 1828, she was welcomed into the 'new spacious dwelling' that had replaced the old building which, some years before, had become rat infested and had deteriorated so badly it had become dangerous. It is not the state of a building that inspires a song of nostalgia and longing, however; it is the bright memories of the folk who there in that linger on. Meanwhile, let the newspaper of the day deal with details that might best be forgotten.

Perthshire Courier **April 29th, 1841**
Rat Killing—On Wednesday the 14th Alexander Menzies, killed in the course of three hours, with his ferrets and terriers, upwards of 200 rats, at Seaside. Mr Hunter of Glencarse, and a number of gentlemen, being on the ground the whole time, and witnessed the extraordinary dispatch of this farmer's greatest enemy. On the 19th, he killed at Mr Kinnear's of Lochtay 120 in one day, with the same dogs and ferrets

Margaret Stewart Simpson
grand-niece of Lady Nairne, Gask, 1894

> My earliest recollections of my Aunt Nairne are of spending
> a winter with her … when I was about seven years old. She
> was very fond of children … we were always allowed by
> her to cut out paper, paste it, paint or make any mess we
> pleased; and we were much annoyed when nurse came in
> and proclaimed that it was bedtime![1]

Christian Murray
Comrie, 2010

> I'm very lucky here—Dalginross House is very cosy and
> they make very good food and they don't fuss you—they let
> you get on with things. I love reading—I would read all day
> long! And I like going for walks—you might be anywhere
> here, in the country, with lovely walks. I don't know who
> used to live here…

Alastair Kissack
Dunira, recorded in Dalginross House, 2008

> **MB:** Alastair, you remember Dalginross when it was a
> house, when a family lived in it?
> **Alastair:** Yes I do. It was Joan Cameron who had it and her
> uncle, a Mr Newbigging. had it before that. He used to live
> in that lovely house at Dalchonzie—he was a bachelor, and
> he had this place too, where he also lived. And then when
> he died he left it to his niece Joan Cameron. An interesting
> thing Joan Cameron told me, was that there was a very
> big firm in Yorkshire called Fairbairn Lawson Combe
> Barbour[2]—a very big firm, in textile engineering. And she

---

1   *The Scottish Songstress: Caroline Baroness Nairne*, p. 30.
2   Fairbairn Lawson Combe Barbour Ltd, textile machinery
manufacturers, National Register of Archives (NRA) NRA catalogue
reference: NRA 14292 Fairbairn Lawson

said, 'Do you know, Alastair, one of the men who started that firm, Fairbairn, was the gardener for my uncle, who owned Dalginross House. He went to a place in Yorkshire and saw the opportunity of this great big engineering firm.' Isn't that interesting? Anyway, it was Mr Newbigging, who lived here—that was a long time ago ... before my time ... my mother and her cousin knew him. He was a very rich old man and the funny thing was, he never married though he loved the company of women but not in that romantic way. He used to give dinner parties, all women, no men there at all, and he liked to give presents. I think he spent much of his life in India, in the East India Company. He had his roots here in Comrie ... it's all history—maybe I should know all this, but I wasn't born in those days. It's a very nice place and it's fascinating all this about past history. But that about Mr Newbigging was quite true—he gave the most lovely jewellery, lovely presents.

Audrey Kissack
Dunira, 2010

Alastair and I knew some that family, in Yorkshire. They lived in a big mansion house called Askham Grange. And, talking of what happens to people's houses—that house is now a women's prison so it is interesting how times change, things change...

Christian Murray
Comrie, 2010

I was born at Pitfour about seven miles from Perth, in Glencarse in 1913. Father's name was Alexander David Murray (the family were Murrays of Scone) and Mother's name was Christian Maule. I don't know where that name came in, it wasn't her maiden name, it was just one of those names. And I was christened Christian Ann Murray and I've got two sisters and a brother. And the brother was much younger, he was six years younger than me, the last of the family. We had very good parents — it's lovely to look back on. We were very carefully looked after at Pitfour and we were so countrified — we didn't have a car. My father wouldn't have a car because he was a farmer and he felt it spoilt the land.

Pitfour was quite a large house, five storeys, with stone stairs — it was just like that picture. My room was right up there, top floor (at the right-hand corner), with 52 steps to go up to my room. All the children slept at the top of the house, under the cupola. I never had a room to myself, always with one of my sisters. Always shared, I took it for granted, I was just one of the three girls, the youngest. Marylou, she was the oldest and she had to have everything very strict, 'don't do this, don't do that!' Then there was Elizabeth — Bessie. And then there was me, then there was a gap and then there was a boy — David. Now all of them are scattered about the place! They all went south — that's going back a bit.

If you look at the photo, the bit that sticks out at the front, that's the library and the music room. And those towers, I remember on some special day they had to go right to the top of the towers and put the flag up. Mother did it, inside the house, up all these ruddy steps and hoisted the flag, the Union Jack.

There was Nanny and there was the governess, and nursery-maid and everybody. And Nanny was always in the nursery. But she didn't sleep there — I don't know where she slept, she was downstairs somewhere. Nanny was always called 'Nanny' but I remember Father coming in to say goodnight to us and he called her Harrison. I remember thinking she could be called *Miss* Harrison.

Miss Reddy was the governess and must have lived in — I don't think she got on with the others, the domestics. They had their little contretemps, I think. I can imagine them all, from the cook downwards — or the cook upwards, should I say? She used to sit in kitchen, in her armchair. I don't think she ever did any work, she directed everyone else! There was the poor girls in the scullery. There was a scullery-maid and a kitchen-maid and the head domestic, the head table-maid. And we were very carefully controlled by them. Oh, yes, we had to do what we were told. There was a big stove in the kitchen, coal, just a stove, iron, nothing fancy, but it kept the kitchen nice and warm. The cat lived in the kitchen, in the basket that used to be for the laundry and the cook sat in her chair and issued orders. 'Do this! Do that! Do the next thing!' We were very frightened of her; in fact we weren't allowed in the kitchen at all, we children were not supposed to be there. It didn't do us any harm! [Laughs] We were very lucky having a nice place to live.

In those days there was no electricity but we made our own gas. The gardener did it out near the stables, in the gas-house, I think it was called—I can smell it now, horrible smell! And there were lamps. One or two had mantles, otherwise it was just the wick—it had to be trimmed. I can't think who did that. And oh yes, the fires always had to be lit. The kitchen was always warm but the house got very cold in winter. The windows would frost over in winter—oh, I can see it even now—jolly cold, but in those days I don't think it ever struck me, it was just the house. We didn't have very good warm clothing, just what Nanny thought was suitable and we didn't always agree with her. We'd have liked something more cosy, like wool, but no, because that would have meant she wouldn't be able to wash it. She was responsible for the washing and drying our clothes. And Nanny's word was law. It's not very nice to be cold but we just took it for granted—that was how we lived, up the stone stairs. And in our bedroom I suppose there was a fireplace but I can't think of one—if there was, it wasn't lit, because that would have been spoiling us. At bedtime there were hot water bottles but Nanny didn't approve. I can see her now, grumpily coming along the corridor with nearly tepid hot water bottles. She thought *that* was spoiling us so she saw to it that they weren't hot.

We looked forward to the summer—that meant you could wear a thin cotton dress and nanny had to provide special knickers that went with that, I think she made them.

We children ate our meals upstairs in the schoolroom with the governess. The house-maid had to carry the meals up the 52 steps, an awful business, up the back stairs too, and it was dark and horrid—then had to carry the dishes down again. For breakfast it was always sausages, nothing else. (No, we didn't have porridge.) And we had tea or cocoa—horrible! I've never forgotten it so I always have tea here, I don't ask for cocoa! I can't remember ever having lunch, but we must have had something. And we had high teas, always—it would be a knife and fork business. We just had to eat what we were given; I don't think we were allowed to choose—except maybe on our birthdays. Scrambled eggs, it could have been, and then steamed puddings—I think we had them every day. The cook would make that in a bowl and you had custard with it.

When we had meals with my parents in the dining-room, that would be a very special day. I sat next to my father—'Behave and use the right knife and fork,' otherwise I was told smartly. For our birthdays the cook would make a cake—it was like a sponge cake and it was covered in icing and blobs of decoration—I can see it now! We seemed to wait ages for one's birthday, for the cake, to see what it was like! [laughs] Sometimes we went to birthday parties—I don't think they came to us, but I think we went to them. I can't remember children coming to us. And at Christmas time there was always parties—they came to us. And the Christmas tree was at the bottom of the stairs—I can see it now!

The New Statistical Account of Scotland, **Comrie, 1845**
A great deal of improvement has taken place in the habits of the people, in respect of cleanliness in their persons and houses; about three-fourths of their homes being slated,

and plastered, and their dress being in general bought, not homespun, as formerly... [3]

Belle Stewart and her daughter, Sheila
Blairgowrie, 1992

Belle: I wis born in a wee bow tent on the bank of the River Tay the 18th of July, 1906—born in a wee bow tent, no doctors, no nurses, nobody, just my aunt, my mother's sister; that was all that was there with her. And my father wis fishin' the Tay at that time, and he got one o the biggest pearls that ever was known up to this day out of the Tay that mornin... Well, when my father got that pearl that mornin he had to walk up to Dunkeld for to sell it to the jeweller.[4] And if he had that pearl the day he could a got a couple o hundred pound for it. An he got either eight or ten pound, I think. I don't reckon he got all that, but anyway, that was a lot of money in his time. And he jist came back to the camp, and I suppose they would hae a dram, but they would celebrate me in some way, you know, the way travellers do, or tinkers, to put it polite—my father was a great tinsmith, he was that; he was really counted among the most skilled craftsmen, but I never knew him because he died when I was seven months old...

Sheila: There wasn't a thing to eat in the camp, or even a drop of tea for the new mother, so when he got the money for the pearl he went to the shop to get food for everyone. And he said to the shop-keeper 'That's two pearls I got the day!' You know, the one he got in the Tay, and his new wee baby.

The New Statistical Account of Scotland, **Killin, 1845**
In the Dochart the pearl muscle [sic, mussel] are found from which beautiful and valuable pearls are extracted...[5]

3   NS, Vol. XI, p. 586
4   Sheila explained that the travelling people often sold their pearls to a chemist since chemists used the same weights for measurement as jewellers.
5   N.S. Vol, X, p. 1081

The New Statistical Account of Scotland, **Errol, 1845**
A broad belting of reeds was planted all along the shores
… they were cut for economical purposes…[for thatching].
These reeds, it may be mentioned were originally planted
by dibbling at the expense of £12 per Scotch acre. The
average produce per acre has been about 500 bundles, each
of 36 or 37 inches circumference. The expense of cutting,
binding, and carrying them out, has been from 3s. 6d. to
4s. per 100 bundles, the rope-yarn being furnished by the
proprietor. The average price at which those of the best
quality have been sold for thatch is £1, 5s. per hundred
bundles; and the price of those of inferior quality, now
chiefly used in covering drains, is about 15s. per 100. The
average number of bundles of both qualities yearly raised
in the parish … was not less than 40,000 bundles.[6]

Allan Walker
Killin, 1964

The houses were all thatched when I was a boy, and then
some o' them that used to be thatched wi' reeds were
latterly covered wi' tin, and now they've got tiles on them
and slates… There's very, very, very little thatching done
now—in fact there's very few that can thatch … I have done
it myself, repairing work, just that only.

It was quite an easy thing to build a house in the olden
times. The way you set about it, well there was four corner
stones, which are big… If we take one at each corner and
then started to build the walls. But first of a' they got what
you call 'roof-trees'. They went to the wood and got trees
with a bend on them at the top, like to fit a roof, eight o'
these. All the ones that I've seen were made of oak, and
roughly hewn by an axe. I don't remember of any Gaelic
word for that, though it was nothing but Gaelic at that time
I don't remember of hearing the word for it 'roof trees'.
Well, it would need to be eight oak trees, [four pairs],

6   N.S., Vol. X, pp. 391-92.

because they had to be joined at the top by wooden pins. When the stonework began, they were built into the wall at the base and curved up.

They were dry stone walls, perpendicular on the outside but the inside, there was a batter on them, which means that the room at the base was much narrower than what it was at the ceiling—there was more width at the ceiling-height, like. The wall was built up to eight feet. And then it was young saplings, probably young larch thinnings, they were laid across these roof-trees on each side and then turf put on the top o' that. They went to the hills—it was tough stuff, you know, they got them in the hills and they covered all the roof wi' that then thatched it, wi' wheat stra' if they could get it—in our time anyway, it was wheat straw. When they got it thatched right up, they put turf on the reeding and cut the turf off, five feet long you know, it was long, narrow strips. It would be anything up to eighteen inches wide and about five feet in length and they laid that on the top o' the thatch o' the reeds and covered the lot with it and at the end it was pegged wi' wooden pegs and battens put across it again, they were either pinned down wi' wood forks—fork pegs—and sometimes there would be wire put across and a heavy stone hung on each end to weight it down and there were larch strips on top of the finished thatch to keep it from getting blown by the wind cos' a high gale would have lifted it up and cleared it all away. Oh yes, it was nothing unusual to see big holes made in the thatch by a high wind. And if it was well done, the thatch would last for several years if it was good stra' they had.

Inside the house there were usually three apartments. We used to call the best end the *seomar*, [the 'room'], the middle one, that's a small one, we called it a closet, *clòsaid*, and the kitchen end was the *ceàrn*.[7]

There was a big, wide chimney but made o' wood, hanging chimney, it was tapered, it went right out through, above the roof, above the rigging, it went straight outside. It

7   Known in Scots as the 'but' end of the house

was wide at the bottom—they were about five feet wide and they came down to about five feet off the floor. They used to burn wood, big logs, and just as it burned away they kept shoving it in. And they used to smoke their hams—there was a big cleek[8] leading to a beam that was across the chimney head, and then there was this long cleek. And attached to that there was a series of round links for to hang your pots on. We used the Gaelic for the chain, of course, that's the *slabhraidh…* There is one, to my knowledge, in the village, beyond the burn—the only one that's left now, but they were in a' these old houses at one time. [9]

The Killin News, No. 21, July 1994
The National Trust for Scotland has recently purchased Moirlanich Cottage, Glenlochay, near Killin and is currently engaged in its restoration…

The National Trust for Scotland, Your Guide 2010
Moirlanich Longhouse, off A827, Glen Lochay Road, near Killin
Get a glimpse of 19th century Scottish Village life in this cottage, which retains many of its original features… Visit this perfectly preserved cruck frame cottage and get a glimpse of Scottish village life in the 19th century. Moirlanich was home to at least three generations of the Robertson family, with the last member leaving in 1968. The building has hardly been changed and retains many of its original features, such as the 'hingin' lum' and box beds. Next door there's an unusual collection of working clothes and 'Sunday best' which were discovered in the longhouse, and an exhibition on the history and restoration of the building.[10]

8   Scots, **cleek**, a hook or crook, often such as is used for hanging meat or a lamp etc. from the ceiling, or for suspending a pot above a fire.
9   School of Scottish Studies Archive, recorded by Dr Anne Ross, (SA1964/18). I am grateful to Iain Walker, grandson of Allan, for permission to publish this excerpt as well as that of Ella Walker, a relative of his grandfather's.
10   Photos and map, http://www.geograph.org.uk/photo/278876

Pat MacNab
Comrie, at the longhouse in Glen Lochay,[11] 2001

When I worked here in 1928, the farmer that was in it had had an accident. He'd broken a leg—Tom Proctor was his name. And they sent for me to come and do the lambin'. Well I'll start at the start, how a came to be here. A letter came to my father askin' could I possibly come up and do the lambin' at *Muirlanich* because he had broken his leg and there was nobody, the other ones were far too old and there was nobody to do it except Tom himself (nephew of the Roberstons who owned the place). So Father said, 'Right I'll send him up.' And these days you communicated by letter so it was a week afore I finally got here. But I left the top of Glenartney in the mornin', and I had to be in Comrie at nine o'clock and I walked the eight miles down from there, caught MacGregors the bakers van from Comrie—they were the bakers and delivered—and they took me to Lix Toll. And old John Robertson met me at Lix Toll, and we walked from Lix Toll (another thee miles) to *Muirlanich*—that was the name of the farm. I don't know how they spell it, but it's always said 'Mu-heer-lan-eech'. And on the road comin' down, John told me about the pearl fishing, and I said 'You're pullin' my leg now!' You know what a young one would be like, an' him wi' the beard—both o' the brothers had beards, and I says 'You're pullin' ma leg noo!'

'No,' he says, 'they make a livin' out o' it, an' everythin' else,' and of course, I didn't believe him, but I soon learned!

So, this is Glen Lochay, right in behind Killin, and it's a lovely glen, and goes right over and over into Glen Lyon.

11   Recorded by MB, Oct. 2001, on a visit with Doris, Pat's son Duncan, Allan Walker and Ewen Sutherland. Allan, who lived in Killin, was the son of the Allan Walker recorded by Dr Anne Ross. He kept the key and welcomed us, being keen to meet Pat as he was a very enthusiastic local historian and regular contributed to the *Killin News*. We were all saddened by his death in December that year.

Today the house has a red tin roof, but in my day it was
a thatched house, and that building over there was the
stables and everything, you see. But this is the house
that I came to when I was sixteen. Come here and I'll
show you ma bedroom! It's on the right as you come in.
Now, there's my bed, the top bunk—that's where I slept,
and Johnny slept there on the bottom, and I went up on
the top. Johnny was a nephew, he was about forty and
he worked on the road—he was separate from the farm.
And he slept in there, and the wee ladder was there—see
the nails o' it? The wee ladder was just enough to get
yourself onto the top. Look at all the layers of all the
wallpapers now! But mind you, it was presentable then—
it wasn't like this!

An' Johnny did the metal for the roads, and shifted
for potholes, and he was away all day. He would rise
wi' me at five o'clock, and sort the horse, feed the horse
you know, and away. And we'd have breakfast—the
cailleach [old lady] made it—she slept in a box-bed in the
kitchen. And we were out o' bed at 5 every morning, and
the cream would be sittin' there in the mornin' on the
bedroom windowsill—it would be skimmed off the top
o' the basin o' milk from the night before. The porridge
was there and the horn spoon—and they always made
the porridge the night before, same thing in Glenartney,
they'd make it and put it in the middle o' hay, on the
kitchen table or somewhere away fae the fire, like a
cosy to keep it warm, in that hay. So it wasn't *hot*, but it
was *warm*. And I carried ma bowl through there to the
kitchen, and ma cream.

Now this is the kitchen—the *cailleach* slept in here, in
the box bed, the warmest place in the house. And she
got out o' bed in the nightie there, bare feet, and she'd
made the breakfast. And the peats were there in beside
the range, though it was logs they used for most o' the
time. It in the morning she just chucked a peat on there,
and the bellows were there, hanging on the wall at the

side, and she'd soon get it going with the bellows. Once
it was going, you wouldn't get near the fire for the heat!
They just cut a log in four or five lengths, and just pushed
it in—and they cut peats as well, for the mornin', to get
the fire going. And see the hingin' lum now—like a
wooden frame—but what's this? *White paper?* Mercy me,
that's been put on lately! That's not the way it was—it
was black, as black wi' the soot. And that's the swee, well,
there's part of it there, it was across there and the kettles
were always boiling, they were just lippin' over.

Now on the windowsill, that was where the cream
was—the window was always open an inch or two, and
the jugs were, and bowls were in there too. And there
was hams hangin' on there, huge hams, and all she'd do
was get out of bed, and get the fryin' pan and the eggs in
there and big slices of ham there, and I had ma porridge
and cream and everything. That wasn't the frying pan
they had in those days; the frying pan' was huge, and she
had the girdle, not that thing [currently on display], she
had a much bigger girdle, and she made the oatcakes
and everything else.

And first thing in the morning, she'd be there in her
nightie, on her bare feet an' everything else, and she just
went through to the hen-house and took the eggs out of
the nest—you'll see the henhouse in minute—and took
the eggs out an' she would knock two eggs in there, and
the ham would be sliced there. She'd get me tae get up
an' get the ham down. An' then once she had me settled,
she'd skip back into bed—still in her nightie!

How old was she? Oh, she was gey near eighty at that
time, I'm sure she was well in the seventies, anyway! And
the brothers, John and Donald they were both elderly
you know, like I mean, I was just a kid compared to them.
The rest of the family were separate, you know, in the
other part of the house—they were the ones in the other
room, with the two box beds, one on each side, in the
sittin' room, as she called it.

And the sheep were in the bottom there. Now they said, 'In the mornin, there'll need to be a bag of Indian corn for the sheep.' It was called at that time—it's maize they call it now. The old folk called it *min Inseanach*[12], aye—and you put on a bag at the back o' the cart, a two-hundredweight bag, and you cut, or unravelled, the end o' the bag, enough to let out a trail o' it, and the horse'll plod on itsel'. You just let the thin line run out—they helped me the first day, but after that you just had to fight your own battles. But anyway, the sheep were properly fed an' everythin'.

So, that was me, five o'clock in the mornin', an' I was away, an' away—yoke the horse, an' got them fed. And I did everythin' an' then I came back in here, had a cup o' tea, an' a went right oot round the top there, an' round the Rigging o' Craignavie, just to make sure there was no sheep because, you see, they were out in the afternoon goin' up through there an' then the came back down to feed. An' any ewe that was lambed up there you see, I found and took back down an' sorted all these things out.

Well then the lambin' went on—I had a great lambin' altogether. I had to lamb very little, an' the only dead lamb I had was one that I tried to twin on there. I lost one ewe an' it nearly broke their heart. That ewe, she hanged hersel' at the back o' the old shed up there. She wasn't that keen on the lamb, so I put her in the corner an' put a sheet o' corrugated iron, like a wee pen, an' in the mornin' when I went o'er, she was lyin' on her back, and hanged o'er the top o' it. Oh mercy, they just went crackers! But never heed! Losin' a ewe, that was just terrible.

So what we did after the lambin', the singles, we drew out, shed—that's parted—all the singles and took them wi' their mothers that were just average age, and able to go—they were fit to go, you know, maybe ten days, or the fortnight, and walked them to Killin, an' put them on

12   Literally, Indian meal.

the train at Killin. And I went with them, and the dog, to Stirling, in the wagon—just stayed in the wagon, oh yes, on my own—I wasn't quite sixteen—fifteen and a half. And then, when we got to Stirling, I drove them up to Speedie's Market, and they were sold there. An' there was nobody to take me home, and Mary Hood, from the Brig o' Lochay, her father was in the Brig' o' Lochay, Mary came for me wi' the big Armstrong Siddeley and took me back home. Well I had two or three jaunts like that—took them to Stirlin' and got them away an' everything else.

And after I finished the lambin' they said, would I not stay and do the ploughin'. So I said, 'Well aye, I could stay,' there was nothing to stop me, an' I was quite happy here, well fed an' everything else. There was always a black-faced wedder, killed and salted at the end of the year you know, it would always be a lamb. So we were very well fed, *very* well fed.

Anyway, I started on the ploughin' and he said, 'Right, I'll put a wheel on to make things easier,' because I'd never—I mean, I'd had shots o' ploughin' over in the glen there wi' old John Smith an' that. An' it was a swing-plough there, an' there was no wheels or anything on. An' he was that bloomin' particular, if you had a little wave in it at all, there was disaster! Anyway, they put a wheel on for me down there, the two horses they had, there was an older mare and this young mare. And he says, 'You'll manage if you're careful with her.' Because I was well accustomed to workin' wi' horses—we'd a hundred an' forty in the glen, and two stallions. An' I was reared frae that height wi' them in Glenartney, and they were let out at ten pounds a week to Ross-shire to Peebles. And they went to all these shootin' places, and that was the bargain, they were away for ten weeks, an' it was ten pounds! But that's getting off the story.

Anyway, I made a start an' got the thing, and I blackened that [field] down there. And I said, 'Who's goin' to sow the corn?'

'Oh, you'll sow the corn!'
'Oh,' I says, 'I've never sowed the corn in my life!'
'Oh,' he says, 'We'll soon sort that!'

And he went an' got the fiddle. Now, they werenae fit to carry it to me, an' Johnny Robertson that was in here, he took the mornin' off, an' I sowed that. An' then I sowed the grass seed as well.

But to get back a bit further; the day that I arrived here, they were splittin' potatoes, up in the barn there, an' they were sittin' on the tub that they had for plotting the pig … an' they had a great heap o' lime on the floor, a depth o' lime, maybe two inches o' lime on the floor, an' when I saw them splittin' their tatties, I'd never seen that done before, like, to that extent, like, I mean—we'd cut potatoes before an' everything else, but they had them like chips! There had to be an eye in every one. The pair o' them, the brothers, they did it. They said, 'Right, we'll need to split open these dreels', an' it was that field, goin' to Daldravaig, at the corner there—that's the field they were in, an' it was Kerr's Pink. So, he got this plough out, an' Johnny came, and between the two o' us, we got it dreeled. And the drills, we ran them at twenty-seven inches. But, like I mean, I'd never done anything like drillin' or anything at that time, but Johnny came along and between us we got it done anyway, got it dreeled. We had a proper dreel plough—it was an Oliver. And we had a swing plough there as well, a lovely swing plough it was, but they fitted this wheel on, you see, to make it easier. It's all these years back, but I could remember the big plough, and it ran the side o' the cut, on the edge, an' you were kept dead right, and if you got the first furrow done right it was effortless. Oh, I did the finishes and everything!

'Right' he said to me, 'into the dung now, an' get carted out. Take that old mare and fill the cart there.' And I wasn't getting time to get the dung spreaded, it was that thick I was howkin' it oot an' back, an' took it along

16

there, an' you never saw dung on the bottom of a dreels like it! And how did the chip potatoes fare? Well, I said, 'I'll come back up in the back end, and I'll see that field.' You never saw a field o' tatties like it! It was absolutely covered in bloom—the whole field! So, whether it was the dung that I put on or no', I don't know, and they were lifted by the time I got back the next time.

So that was the potatoes, and then the corn though I wasn't here when the corn, the oats, was harvested. And they sowed the grass seed, and that was out, it was a big bit o' land. And he had a bloomin' dog here, oh, he was a bad bugger, he was—he was a black, bear-skinned dog, an' one day we were down there an' the dogs were runnin' loose there, an' he ran an' chased a ewe in at the swing bridge. An' she was floatin' about in the middle of the river, in the big pool at the swing bridge, and of course, I wasn't goin' in after her, so the poor beast was drowned. So he got locked up—I took him away home an' locked him up, but I don't know whether it belonged to Tom, him wi' the broken leg, or whether it was him let him run on any road he liked, I don't know. So that was that!

Socialising? I didna have time to think, never mind do any socialising! I was workin' night an' day here, graftin' there from mornin to night. Well, it was just myself and everything had to be done. And the cows were through in the byre there, but the brothers took in the cows. I had nothing to do with the cows, and muckin' the byre; one of the brothers did the milking. And the hens, they went out o' that wee hole out there.

In those days it was all horses here. I didn't have to shoe any because they were shod when I came here. And of course they were horsey folk anyway, the Robertsons themselves. They had an light-legged one they used in the gig—a light-legged beastie it was, and that's when they went visitin'; they went away in that machine [gig] down that farm, then away down near the loch, after you go up the brae out to Killin, and go down the loch-side, and it goes away down like an' avenue for miles, away down to the bottom. I remember goin' down there two or three times wi' them—it would be near Morenish, but it's right away down near the loch, the place was that we went to.

Johnny's horse was a light brown, and it wasn't a pure Clydesdale, there was a bit o' something else in it, because it wasn't as big, for that part o' it. He had it in the cart. Mind, he did the metal for the roads, shifted for potholes, and he was away all day. And they themselves had two mares, both Clydesdales. One was an older beast—she was the one we had for the ploughin'. But the young one, the black mare, she was my pride and joy! She was beautiful mare, a Clydesdale and I got on great with her. I used to wash her legs at night and take all the dirt off and everything else – she was black wi' white socks.

Anyway, this day they were away, there was nobody here, and I had a notion: I got hold of a saddle in there, and the cart was out at the corner, wi' a stob holdin it up, so I took her down, got the britchen on, and I backed her in, and I brought it down just gently, and got round and got her all hooked up, and I just took her by the mouth, you know, to start with—led her by the side of her jaw, and she went away as right as rain. And I thought whenever she hit the roadside that there would be too much of a rattle—but no, was there what! She did great altogether, so I went away along, walked her away along to Daldravaig, then said to myself, 'To hang wi' this!' An' I got up on the cart, and I came back down the road and they were here—the family had returned home! Well they nearly ate me, I tell you!

There was nothing about 'boys will be boys' then, but 'that's a valuable beast! And if anything had happened...' This is what they were on about! They were shocked, because I don't think any of the brothers wanted to put her in the harness themselves. Well from that day she was on the cart, and that was her, broken in! And it was me that broke that mare in, and everythin' that was done about her. We fed them pure oats, and locust beans[13], and they grumbled about me feedin' the horse too much! Eventually the black mare was sold to Black, o' Collessie in Fife. And the Blacks are still great horsemen yet, and they're always showin' Clydesdales yet. And she was sold for a hundred pounds—a lot of money in those days—and it was me that broke her in.

I was in *Muirlanich* from the beginning of March to the end of June, because they were waiting on me to get back to the shooting at Glenartney. Oh life was good—see we didn't know any better—or worse! And there was a contentment—we were country born and bred, an' used to doin' a lot o' things about the glen an' all. And these days, you were young, and there's nothin'll stop you. And, *Muirlanich,* was the name of the farm, but after years and years, I found out that the National Trust (who took it over) had called it *Moirlanich.* How they shifted it I do not know.

Looking at the maps...

The National Trust Property bears the name that appears on all Ordinance Survey maps from 1861 to the present day. See OS Sheet LXVIII14 (Kenmore Det. No. 1), scale 25 inch to the mile, 1898—99, 2nd edition, 1901, Grid reference: NN562341. John Stobie's much earlier map of 1783, however, has Muirlanich, which crucially has a 'u' not 'o'

---

13   The term 'locust beans' refers to the seeds of carob pods, which look rather like broad beans. They are harvested from the carob tree, an evergreen tree native to Mediterranean and Middle Eastern regions. As it is sweet to taste, the carob is better known as a sugar or chocolate substitute, often used in cakes, while the seeds, the locust beans are used for animal food. John the Baptist's subsistence on 'locusts and wild honey' (Matthew 3:3) and the Prodigal son's diet of locusts (Luke 15:16) would have been much more appetizing than we might have imagined.

as the second letter.[14] Bearing in mind that map-makers relied entirely on local residents to tell them local place-names, and that Perthshire was entirely Gaelic-speaking at the time, the sound was written down using English orthography as few map-makers could speak Gaelic, far less write it. Pat's pronunciation resonates entirely with the Gaelic sounds, as the first four letters are pronounced as two syllables, and not as a diphthong, which would be an English convention. Thus, Pat's pronunciation of the letters 'M-u-i-r' is in two syllables, 'Mu' and 'ir', sounding like 'muh-hear'. Later map-makers rendered these two letters as 'oi', producing a diphthong and creating an entirely Anglicize sound, 'moir'. Folk such as Pat, who listened to the family whose home it had been for three generations, had no need of maps, and neither did the Robertsons, whose home it had been three generations. Their knowledge of oral tradition far exceeded that of the 'official guides'.

Queen Victoria, Saturday, September 10, 1842[15]

We passed Killin, where there is a mountain stream running over large stones, and forming waterfalls. The country we came to now was very wild, beginning at Glen Dochart, through which the Dochart flows; nothing but moors and very high, rocky mountains. We came to a small lake called, I think, Laragilly, amid the wildest and finest scenery we had yet seen. Glen Ogle, which is a sort of long pass, putting one in mind of the prints of the Kyber Pass, the road going for some way down hill and up hill, through these very high mountains, and the escort in front looking like mere specks from the great height.

---

14   I am grateful to staff at the National Library of Scotland map-room, particularly Tam Burke, for helping me with this search.
15   Leaves from the Journal of Our Life in the Highlands... (London: Smith, Elder, 1868)

Mary Mathieson
Lochearnhead, 2010

I was born in a croft in Glen Ogle just before the end o'
the First World War, 1918. There were twelve in the family
and I was the second last. The name of the croft is *Taigh na
Mhuillean*. Now you know that's the mill house. My father
spoke Gaelic. Fluent Perthshire Gaelic—his name was
Donald Kennedy. My mother didn't have Gaelic—she was
Mary MacLellan and she came from Roseneath. Her father
was a carter to Princess Louise's daughter, that's them who
had a castle, and my grandfather was a carter, what we
would now call a lorry driver. My mother had people in
Islay and they had Gaelic.

And in those days, Glen Ogle was a crofting area, so we
grew up with it—every stage of crofting. My mother and
father had cows, and they used to sell the milk. And we
used to take the milk in the cans down as we were going
to school and hand them in the station cottages right down
to our customers. And then after school, when we were
finished at four o'clock we collected empty cans again.
People usually paid every week, in those days it was
fourpence a pint.[16] We usually had about five milkers
and there was young ones as well, the followers. And my
mother did all the milking—she did that. I think women
did most of the work in the croft. Now forby
doing your own cows' milk, my mother used
to go up and do Glen Ogle Farm's milking.
And it was a wee job for her, it was a wee
wage, and she left the money, she didn't lift
it, she left it. Then maybe in six months she
would lift it and buy shoes or boots for her children. She
was the dairy-maid for Glen Ogle Farm—that would be
maybe ten minutes walk from us, so she'd start early, maybe
six o'clock in the morning and go up there for the milking.

---

16   In present currency, that's just over one and a half pence a
pint.

It's quite early but I think she would do our own first and then theirs and that would be a bigger lot than the five of her own. Oh, yes, that would be a lot, and then she would go back up at night and milk again. She started as a dairymaid at the Lochearnhead Hotel anyway—that's how she started milking.

My father used to be a ploughman for the hotel, as well as the croft. He would do part-time for the hotel— that's how they met, when she was the dairymaid. I suppose he would start that when he was a young man, before he took over the croft, and he was a good ploughman—he got a prize for being the best ploughman when he was young.

Then when my mother came and they married, they stayed with her mother-in-law, and my mother had to learn all the ways of the croft. My father got a job wi' the railway and my mother was the one that run the croft. Now, you didn't own the croft, and you didn't own the house—you paid a rent to the Breadalbanes, then it was the Camerons (the ones that had the Lochearnhead Hotel). And one day there had been a shoot and my mother went down to the field and she found a pheasant that had fallen so she took it home, very pleased with herself. And my father gave her an awful row, he said 'Never, ever do that again or we would be put out the house if it was found out that we lifted a pheasant!' The pheasant was dead anyway, but no, never do that! She thought she was doing all right, but that was a lesson to her. Shame, that great control on a woman, eh? Of course my father used to snare rabbits—you could do a lot of that on your own ground. He'd tell us to keep an eye on them when he was away to work, and what did we do? We let the rabbits go! (laughs)

There were twelve of us, that's twelve pairs o' hands— they'd all be needed when we were plantin' potatoes. My father still did the ploughing—I remember one year when he got a prize for being the best ploughman. And do you know what the prize was? The prize was a big bag of tatties! Was that no' a good prize! And they were good potatoes too—the very best, the very best. I like the Edzell Blue myself, but you don't much get them now.

Perthshire Advertiser, 6th October 2010

A purple potato that growers claim contains greater health benefits than the average white variety is to go on sale… The 'Purple Majesty' has a deep purple skin and flesh and contains nine to 10 times more antioxidants than standard potatoes … the potato was bred from a traditional variety by scientists at Colorado University, but trials over the last two years found it could be grown in Scotland. Supermarkets are soon to stock the deep purple potatoes grown in Perthshire…

Mary Mathieson

And as well as potatoes we'd carrots and everything on the croft. The cooking as well as everything else was done in the kitchen—we'd a grate in the kitchen, an open fire, and it was mostly wood—it got too hot in the winter. There was peat too and we bought a whole lot of coal. The hotel people used to get a big wagon of coal, and the crofters got their share. We paid for it of course—the Camerons, Ewan's father, would order it. There was an old lady who lived beside us, in fact she's in the house, a single house that was up the croft to the left hand side—and she lived alone. Her husband was killed in the First World War, and we were told to go up and get water for her, help her, you know. And when the coal came outside the door, we had to take her coal in, into the house, the bottom of her bed, on the floor 'cause she was goin' about on two sticks. So we had to help her to get the coal in, she gave us sixpence each. And she made tea in the skillet, you know what that is? That's a wee pan, on the open fire. There was plenty sticks round about, always plenty, but of course you couldn't just cut whatever wood that you liked, just trees that had come down themselves, windfalls and rubbish we found lying about. We used to go up, across the burn and get sticks, after I come home from school and had a piece then we'd go up and get sticks for the fire.

Most o' the time my father was working on the railway—he was watchman in Glen Ogle and it would be about two miles, anyway, before he would get a start for the day. There were three watchmen and they had a hut—up near that viaduct there.[17] And inside the hut they had a paraffin lamp and there was a wee stove. And the rail men provided the coal—loads of coal, the best of coal thrown off to the boys, so they would never be cold, never! I remember my father was well shod, wi' good leggings too and good coat. And in a bad winter with that long walk in the snow he would have to make it some way or another, just walk through it—wi' leggings you see, they would cover his boots—but he always got there.

And there were three shifts, one the early morning, from six o'clock to two, the other one from two o'clock till ten and the next one was from nine o'clock at night till six in the morning. That's the three shifts. So, there was a wee overlap the nine to ten one, you could get a wee yarn, a wee brew up. But it must have been lonely sometimes, don't you think? I often think that. You read a lot though, but then you had to walk to watch for the trains. He had to walk the length, and he called it 'The Length'.

They had a lamp of the different colours; you know he'd turn it red, and blue for the signals to the train. And he carried fog signals in his pocket, for, say a rock came down on a line, he would put down his fog signals on the line, and that's a warning to the engine driver to look out for danger. It went off, like shots

---

17   The twelve-arch viaduct was built as part of the railway line connecting Callander and Oban, through Glen Ogle and the Pass of Brander. The line was closed during the Beeching cuts in the early fifties.

wi' the train going over them. They would put them down a good bit away, so he would walk a good bit away from where the rock fell, to give them a chance, maybe a mile up the track, and one of these would go off, the driver would stop, by the time he reached it. That's what he did and he always kept pockets of that stuff, kind of gun powdery stuff—we called them fog signals. There was a bunk in the hut, but you wouldn't be getting any sleep—you'd be watching. There was the phone as well, you see, so you would have to phone up to Glen Ogle Head, and keep in touch. One of these wind up ones, crank, crank, crank.

You know what we liked? We liked it when he forgot his sandwiches and we had to go up the railway, up to the hut, and he would make us tea. He used to make jam, strawberry jam, wi' the wild strawberries just outside his door. There were blaeberries up there too—oh, I love the blaeberries. He'd make a wee pot for himself. Just for his piece, there wouldn't be enough to take home, there would only be enough for just a wee drop at a time. And then he would see us on the road again. 'Watch the trains! Run down the bank if you hear a train coming,' he used to say. 'Don't let them see you. You have to run down the bank.' *We were the railway children!* We used to take the goats under the bridge, and the train would be coming and we'd be runnin' down, and we'd be waving to them, the engine driver, and the driver; and the visitors and the passengers would be sitting dining and we'd be waving to them.

And while he was on the railways, jumping shifts, my mother did everything else. Of course we all helped and in the summertime we used to take the cows up the railway. You see where that railway was there? Well, there's a viaduct, and we used to go right up, along, up though the wee bridge up there. Put the cows up there and shut the gate. That was for the summer pasture—to the *aighrean*. Remember you did that, the sheilings? Well, there's still ruins yet up there. But in my father's and mother's day there was nobody stayed overnight in the *airigh*, no, no.

My mother kept poultry, she would raise them from the eggs and she'd a lovely big turkey-hen, it was called 'The Incubator'! And she used to lay away up the burn. She'd make a nest for herself wi' what ever could she find, bracken and a lovely camouflage, by the burn-side, near the waterside where she could get a drink—beautiful, just beautiful. And she'd lay a lot of eggs and bring the wee turkeys out—sometimes we got to see them hatching. Beautiful! And that was down by the old mill—I was telling you about the mill.

Then we had pigs—two pigs were kept all summer. There was a sty and pen, as well, and it had a sink and everything for the water. We had lovely pig houses—one for the boy pig and one for the girl pig. My father made them out of a sleepers, you know what sleepers are? They're from the railway—aren't they lovely? And sometimes when the soo wid have piglets, among the litter there would be the wee delicate pigs used to come tae us, to keep them warm. And we used to look after them, bring them into the house, just like lambs, put them in a box near the fire to keep them warm—till they were stronger, so the soo widnae trample them. But when it came to the end of the summer, they were ready to go to market, one pig was sold, and the other pig, I'm afraid, was used for the home—it's sad, we didn't keep the piglets. Well we had to sell them—it was our living, you see. And the geese used to go to the markets as well and the turkey, but there was always one turkey left for us for Christmas.[18]

The New Statistical Account of Scotland, 1844—45
... Glenogle, signifying the terrific glen is a narrow pass leading from Lochearnhead ... it is surrounded on both sides of the road by stupendous hills full of rocks and

---

18   As this book was going to press, we were saddened at the news of Mary's death, Nov. 9, 2010. May these pages be as stones on her cairn.

scarnachs, the haunts of foxes and ravenous birds ... [It
is in] the parish [of Balquhidder] about 18 miles in length,
and between 6 and 7 miles in breadth, and comprises a
good many straths, glens, and valleys, and a vast number
of hills and lofty rocks...[at] Lochearnhead... there is
a small country village with a good inn, having every
requisite accommodation for travellers...

Above the manse [in Balquhidder] is a stupendous
rock, much admired by all travellers and seen at a great
distance.[19]

Robert Tannahill (1774—1810), c. 1800

Will ye go, lassie, go, to the Braes o' Balquhidder
Where the blaeberries grow, 'mang the bonnie bloomin' heather...

The Old Statistical Account of Scotland, **Balquhidder, 1792**
The number of horses is about 170; of black cattle, about
800; and of sheep, 18,000. The sheep are mostly of the
strong black faced south country breed ... the average
price of white wool unwashed, for some years past, is 7s.
3d per stone...

...upon each farm, besides the tenants, there are one
or two cottagers consisting of weavers, taylors, dyke-
builders, and old women.* There is 1 writer in the parish;
and 3 students of philosophy from it attend the college of
Glasgow.

> *Most of the tenants keep a maid-servant for the purpose of*
> *spinning woolen and linen yarns for cloathing [sic] the family, and*
> *for sale... There are few men-servants employed excepting herds,*
> *who from besides their maintenance, are allowed for their wages or*
> *fee to keep from 40 to 60 breeding ewes with their master's flock,*
> *the profits of which are from £8 to £15 sterling commonly...*

...the common language of the people is Celtic[†], but most
(if not all of them) can buy and sell and transact business
with their low country neighbours in English.

---

19   Statistical Account 1834-45 vol.10 pp. 348-349

†Mr Robert Kirk, one of the incumbent's predecessors, gave the first version of the psalms in the Gaelic language.

Peat is the only fuel used here … most inhabitants carry some coal from Bannockburn, a distance of about 30 miles. … the people are, in general, lively, intelligent, fond of news and hospitable to strangers. Few of them are rich and not many of them are poor…[20]

Jean lnnes

Balquhidder, 1990:

I was born in 1900, May 22, in the Braes of Balquhidder. I was christened Jean MacNaughton and in those days we had to be christened at home because it was difficult taking a baby in a horse-drawn vehicle down to the kirk in the village. Inverlochlarig is at the far end of the Braes. The name Balquhidder is from Gaelic, *Baile-chuil-tir*, meaning 'the distant farm'. Inverlochlarig was chiefly a sheep farm—goes away west towards Loch Lomond-side and north towards Crianlarich and then over to Loch Katrine-side there—about 10,000 acres. (It's been in the family since 1877). And nowadays they tell us we're in Stirling! We shouldn't be in Stirling! We should be in West Perthshire because the farm actually marches with part of Loch Lomond-side.

Father managed the farm—he had cattle too. To begin with it was Highland cattle—I can remember a lot of Highland cattle and then they went to Aberdeen Angus—around sixty, perhaps; we'll have about a hundred now. And oh, they had a lot of sheep—thousands. And they would have perhaps seven shepherds, a man for the horses, and an 'odd person' [an orraman]. But that's in the old days; now they don't have that. If they were hiring, that was usually in May and November, these two term days, Whitsuntide and Martinmas, the 28th of May and the 28th of November, and that would be in Perth or Stirling. I think they called it a feein' market or a hiring fair. Of course then it came about that they heard of shepherds you know. And at the hiring they usually got a two-and-six (half-crown) in their hand—I don't know what they called it, but they got that[21]—to seal the contract, as it were. Though that need only be for the six-month term it was understood that unless they were hopeless, that they'd stay indefinitely. And they did at the Braes—they were all twenty years, most of them. Then they heard of men if they were going about—it wasn't a case of always hiring people in the year or every two years.

The Glen was full of Highlanders—all Gaelic-speakers. For the unmarried shepherds they had what was called a bothy. In the Braes it was quite a big bothy and they had a housekeeper. Well there would be three or four bedrooms and a kitchen and there was another room. Of course Rob 's old house is still there, but this was built onto—they made rooms off it, you see. The house that Rob Roy lived in and died in, (1774), that's been done up now and it's let to people. Oh it's an awfully nice place. Well, we didn't make an awful lot of that in our day—you took him for granted. People regarded him as a Robin Hood. He was supposed to have been a wild man, stealing and that, but he wasn't really. He stole, but according to the standards of the district he wasn't worse than anybody else, and he always worked for the poor, he upheld them, you see—a sort of Scottish Robin Hood.

There were no tractors of course! The horses had to do all these things so we had two or three big horses—they weren't as big as Clydesdales—and we'd a pony for going up and down with the gig. So there was a horseman and he lived with the shepherds. And he had a hill too, to look after. He was a shepherd-cum-horseman, or a horseman-cum-shepherd. Of course the married ones had their own place. And the shepherds kept dogs—they had at least three

21   In some areas, known as the 'arles'.

dogs each. Oh well, they would need them for these hills, you know. They would have two working and one going out or coming in, you know. And there were kennels for the dogs and each man looked after his own dogs.

The dairy was part of the house at the Braes. I milked for years and years and years—oh it was a grand job, hand-milking, I liked it. Well, the women did it a lot—oh yes, men didn't like milking, really. We milked at seven in the morning and seven at night, three cows for the house, and we did two for the bothy, night and morn. And you'd carry the pails straight from the byre to the dairy—no electricity in those days, but you could still keep everything cool, even in summer. You see, the dairies were very carefully built. They'd stone shelves and stone floors. The stone shelves had places underneath for all the dairy things. And in some, in most farm-houses on the Braes, nothing was built above them. They were very cool places; they faced north-east, it was pretty cool. There was one, two, three big windows, one to the north and two to the east. So even when you walked in during summer it was cool, oh yes. The roof was slated. But there were no bedrooms above the dairy part of the house.

Then straight from the byre, the milk went through a sieve, we called it, with two copper things at the bottom of it, one with bigger holes and another one with smaller. And in the old days, all the milk went into great basins and on the stone shelves it would cool and, say, this morning's milk would be there till tomorrow morning, and then the cream was skimmed off. We used a flat thing, (what was it called? a skimmer), it was an iron one—you're supposed to have holes in it, but ours didn't have holes in it. You had just to be careful you didn't take a lot of milk, you see.

But oh it was great! They talk about porridge now, porridge and *milk*, but we never had *milk* with our porridge! I still have the big jug—this size, blue and, oh, blue rings round it, and that was filled with cream. Of course there was seven of us—five of us children and father and mother, seven, and that was to the top with cream! And that was what we had every morning for breakfast—cream and porridge. And now the authorities are telling us we shouldn't eat cream! I don't know how some of us are alive still! [Laughs] For ninety years![22]

And we made all our own butter in those days. We had a fairly big churn (about 3 feet high)—you could get bigger ones. Ours was a medium sized one; it wasn't the very small one. And then it had the wee window you looked in at, and it had the place where you put the water in. It was suspended on a trestle, and it went head over heels, you know ... it was like a barrel; it went head over heels, you see you turned this handle. And we made butter once a week, or once in ten days, perhaps. And oh, there was salted butter—we had big crocks. You know these lovely big earthenwares? We'd salt it and press it in—so it would keep for the winter. It was quite a lot of work, but oh it was beautiful butter.

Eventually we got a cream separator, oh, early 1930s— that's another story altogether! This was before I was married, at the Braes, and the first time we used that separator I didn't go to church in the morning; I spent Sunday morning putting that separator together. And we didn't know anything about separators. And oh, we had quite a reception! My brother Alastair was there, his wife Ann was there and mother was there, and we'd a very nice girl, Bessie from—I forget the other name—she was there and we were all watching. And you had to turn it so often a minute, you see, and quicker and quicker, round and round and round. Suddenly there was the most unearthly explosion! Something must have been touching something it shouldn't have been and it went up like that, and all the milk was in the container. And this bowl came out and it was dancing around the stone floor all over the place. And it hit mother there (on her leg)—she had a sore leg for a

22   Jean lived another seven years, till 97.

long time. And it hit Bessie somewhere in the middle; she fainted. And Alastair had on a new suit and his wife had tried to get him to change his suit before he came up; he was living down, he was living here—and his suit was saturated with milk. And I was hit there (on the head and the shoulder). And I had on a jersey—I think it was winter, and whole pieces were taken out it! Well we'd an awful job! And of course the separator was all in a hundred bits. And we were going off with the eggs the next day, Ann and I. Things were very bad, it was in the early '30s and we kept hundreds of hens and we would hawk these eggs round on a Monday and we had these thirty dozen cases filled with the eggs, and they were underneath—I told you there was a place underneath the shelves, and of course some of them were soaked. Oh, I didn't get to bed till five o' clock the next morning. However, to cut a long story short, we got over that difficulty. And it was guaranteed, if anything went wrong, so I wrote away and said that ... I just said— anyhow, oh in the finish they said, oh, they would give us another one, but it would be smaller. But of course it was a smaller one we wanted. It was too big, the one I got. So, we got a smaller separator, and we had it, it was there when Jeananne came. But that's the story of the separator. It was very good. Oh they were very good things, the separators. They came from Kilmarnock, I think. They had all the dairy things, the westies, the folk in Ayrshire. Anyway, the separator was very good.

And that did away with all these basins of milk left out, but of course we kept the milk we wanted—that didn't go through the separator. You had to be very careful washing the milk things, though. You'd to wash them in cold water first, and then in warm, and then they were all scalded with a boiling kettle. You carried it from the scullery which was next door—mind, the dairy was part of the house at the Braes. And the kitchen had a big grate, you know— wonderful grates they were! There was never any trouble about frozen pipes. There was this huge grate in the kitchen, and that had a lovely fire, and it had a hood that went in or came out—you could have it an open fire or you could push that back, and it was just lovely. And it had a wee boiler at the side, and that heated water. And they got water from there, and of course the kettles, they had huge big iron kettles, you know, black kettles, and they were always sitting on the hobs. You first took the kettle out. There was a slatted bench outside the back door against a wall, and in summer all the milk things went out there and they were scalded out there and cooled. Oh it was wonderful. And the skimmed milk, well, it went to animals and it went to different things.

And I'll tell you another thing, there was a hostel down at Monachyle, and people from Glasgow and Edinburgh stayed there and they used to come up for milk. Well, we only had separated milk, and they used to take it, but they knew it was separated—we didn't measure what we gave them, and they came to the door. Now if it was the 'Edinburgh (holiday) weekend' or the 'Glasgow weekend' we knew there would be a lot of folk, and we gave them so much in their cans. They all knew, and we had a box and they put in what they liked—a penny or tuppence. They would go hill-walking and they all came on bicycles or on their feet; there were no cars. There were a lot of students, Edinburgh and Glasgow students—we knew a lot of them.

At the beginning of winter you'd need to buy stuff in. We had what we call a kist in the kitchen—two divisions, and that was fumigated in November. And we got flour and we got oatmeal; I forget how much, but one side was flour and other side oatmeal. And they came from D. & J. MacEwen. He didn't come regularly but he used to come up to the Braes and we got two hundredweight of sugar, that's a barrel of sugar—we got the flour and the oatmeal and sugar. And there was a big thing of rock salt and it was hung up in the kitchen, a block of salt, covered with paper. And that's what was used for the salt butter, you see.

And in those days, of course, we'd no electricity. We

had lamps—paraffin lamps, to begin with—there were no Aladdins or Tilleys; that came much later, but paraffin lamps with the wicks and globes, you know. It was quite a job doing them—they had to be done very particularly, and where the wicks came up they were polished. Oh, they were kept very meticulously; we had one, two, three, four, five, six, and then three wee lights. The paraffin came from Balquhidder Station—we bought a great big drum, a red drum. And it did the whole winter.

And then we made our own candles. Well in November they killed fat sheep. A *fat* sheep—they wouldn't be used today! And father used to go in and look at them if he hadn't been in at the picking of them all, when he was older, in the dairy, you see, they were hung up and they were opened out. And if they weren't fat enough, it would be 'Who chose this one?' There'd be an awful row! But they were the fattest sheep they could get. And all the fat that wasn't used for, well, it was used in white pudding, and it was used in haggis, different things, the rest was all boiled down for candles. And it was put in great big pots and that was sitting on the grate and then that was sieved into basins and left. And then when it got hard you scraped the foot [of the block of lard]. And that was done three times. And then it came out all pure, and that was rolled in paper and put in a barrel, a wooden barrel. And that was the candle fat.

Then late in November, or the beginning of December, on a day when there wasn't much wind, the night before there'd be a huge big pot sitting on the grate. And the pot was sitting there and all the fat melted. And there was another great big pot and it was in the middle of the floor— the floor was covered with paper and it was in the middle of the floor, and there was a trestle went from one end, from the pot to that end, and one from this end—two bits of stick and they were sticks over it with wicks hanging. We'd prepared all this the night before. There were eight wicks on each stick. They were about that [two inches] apart, you see; you'd to allow for the candles to grow—eight wicks were cut, and that was along there, four there and four there, just what you could reach from a chair in the middle. And somebody made a wee chair for me at the end, and I had two wee sticks—when I was very wee.

I remember it took the whole day. The big pot was filled with boiling water that was kept topped up with boiling water, and then the grease on top of it. Boiling grease from the thing, and it was lifted over in a scoop, you know, with a pail and kept topped up, and you dipped these in, you see, the wicks. Sticks in and out, and in and out, and in and out, and so the candles grew. And you see you would have eight eights, that's sixty-four. You would have a lot of candles. Magical watching the candles growing out of pieces of string? I don't remember that—I took it for granted, you just took it for granted.

They had a pleasant smell. Oh, they were good candles. And then they were left there for a day and they were left another day; they had to be really hard. And they were in boxes like this [about a foot square]. And then put away in newspaper, and then the next row was put, and so on until you got up the top; and the whole thing was covered, the sides and the bottom and the top, with newspaper because of the mice—if you put newspaper in, the mice didn't go for them because they didn't like the print, the ink. And that box of candles went up into the loft—we'd an attic upstairs, a big loft, and the candles were kept there; I remember the very place.

Cameron Clark, age 8
Errol, 2010

My granddad Harry Clark is eighty-nine and my great-great-uncle Greg Malloy is eighty-four and three-quarters. I heard from them that Errol got its electricity supply in 1944. One lady thought this was great, cos she could see to light her candles!

Dorothy Wordsworth,
Balquhidder, 13 September 1803[23]

Our guide had been born near Loch Voil, and he told us that at the head of the lake, if we would look about for it, we should see the burying-place of a part of his family, the MacGregors, a clan who had long possessed that district, a circumstance which he related with no unworthy pride of ancestry. We shook hands with him at parting, not without a hope of again entering his hut in company with others whom we loved….

The lake is divided right across by a narrow slip of flat land, making a small lake at the head of the large one. The whole may be about five miles long.
As we descended, the scene became more fertile, our way being pleasantly varied - through coppices or open fields, and passing farm-houses, though always with an intermixture of uncultivated ground. It was harvest-time, and the fields were quietly—might I be allowed to say pensively— enlivened by small companies of reapers. It is not uncommon in the more lonely parts of the Highlands to see a single person so employed. The following poem was suggested to William…

Behold her single in the field,
Yon solitary Highland Lass,
Reaping and singing by herself
Stop here, or gently pass.
Alone she cuts and binds the grain,
And sings a melancholy strain.
Oh! listen, for the Vale profound
Is overflowing with the sound…

---

23   *Recollections of a Tour Made in Scotland 1803*

Jimmy Stewart
Locherlour, 2009

I was born in Callander in 1921, on a small farm, just up
from the Falls of Lenny. My elder brother was the third
generation—my sister always maintains that he was the
fourth generation—on the small farm. I'd just left school,
February the 5th was my birthday, and I never went back—I
said, 'to hell with it, I'm off!' So, I started workin' small
farms—there were a lot of dairy farms in those days—
milkin' cows, doing some agricultural work, ploughing,
working a pair of horses when I was 15 year old. Aye, a pair
of horse at fifteen year-old! And then I left one or two other
places because the sheep was what I preferred. So in 1936, I
got the chance to go to Balquhidder to a Mr and
Mrs MacIntyre—*Immeroin* was the name of the
place. And the first thing I did was I got to milk
the cows all the time! And then I was on to the
small hirsel[24] full of sheep, in what they call *Glen
Sionach*. And then after three years the boss said to me, he
says 'I'm puttin' ye on to the big hirsel, the Grachler.' What's
the English for that? A green hill. And of course the glen,
Glen Buckie, started from the bottom of Loch Voil, right
up to the top end of Immeroin Farm. So I was there for ten
year. I met my wife and that was that. She didn't grow up
there, but her forebears were from Balquhidder—previous
to that, her grandfather was the precenter in the church in
these days, in Balquhidder.

And there was quite a few Gaelic speakers in the area—
the Fergusons had very good Gaelic… At that time the glen
was a community. And I've seen us leaving Gartnafuaran at
11 o clock at night after playing 'catch the ten'! Och, drams
flowing of course! (Laughs) Aye, and then sometimes up
to the knee in snow and two and a half mile to walk home!

---

24   A flock of sheep amounting to the number of sheep looked
after by one shepherd or on one small farm; also refers to an allotted
area of pasturage to be grazed by a flock.

You ever thought anything about it—just young and daft—
and fit! And across on the other side of Loch Voil, the Braes
of Balquhidder, oh, I remember 'Jean the Braes', they used
to call her.

In those days now, there was no shop in Balquhidder, but
a post office only, and Mistress Moir kept it—she was one of
the old glenners, oh, a topper of a lady altogether. Many's
a ceilidh we had in the house too! It was at the crossroads
there below the church, the post office also sold cigarettes
and tobacco and stuff like that, and other essentials. I can
still see us going down late at night, maybe after lambing,
for a packet of cigarettes or something, 'Oh just come away
in, you better have a dram before you go up that bad road
again.' You know, that was the homeliness about her.

There was a wee shop in Balquhidder Station, miles
away, the Macdonalds, and that was the only shop. But of
course there was vans in these days, oh yes there was
vans. But these were the happy days I can assure
you. And you would stock up for the winter, but on
a sheep farm you didn't need a butcher's van. And
at Immeroin the lady of the house was a tremendous cook,
and when there was a sheep slaughtered for the house
there was not a thing missed. Sheep's head broth, there was
the blood used for puddings—the *marags*—oh yes, it was
all used, none wasted. Tripe, a regular thing, yes, kidneys,
everything. Butter was made just about twice a week, there
was two cows heavy with milk at the time. They were well
fed and looked after, I mean nobody was hungry. We had
hare for hare soup, oh, I'd be sent away with the gun to
get a pair of hares and that would be quite enough. And
they were hung for a few days and that was it. And what
they did with the hares in those days was, they boiled the
hare with the soup, took the hare out, it was all in parts of
course, and then it was roasted in the oven. It was beautiful,
you know, and it had that we crust on it. And we grew
our own potatoes and everything, Kerr's Pink and Golden
Wonder. Oh we were never hungry—the advantage of

having a sheep farm was you were never hungry!

And you did everything needed doing—lambing, marking, dipping, clipping, getting ready for the sales. Every farm had it's own brand—and they still do. They have the initials of the name of the place, say, *Ballimore*, *Immeroin* or the initials of the owner, and some have the year the lambs were born. I always do the year, so if you take lambs that were born this year [2009], when they come home from the wintering, there would be a 9 on the horn brand. And you put a keel mark on them as well, on the wool—the different colours of keel—I used mostly red, and you would remember everybody's marks. When I was younger, there were a lot of good boys among sheep in them days, let me tell you, and to get up beside them, you had a bit of doing! We'd all be at the fank, you would just come into a pen, sometimes in the shedder—d'you know what I mean by stragglers and shedders? A straggler, that's sheep that doesn't belong to you—they coudnae find the mother of it, so you didn't know who owned it. And the 'shedder' is the narrow passage between the pens—usually had a pivot gate. So you'd take hold of the stragglers and at the shedders and I used to point to the pen, when they were going through the shedder. And the person there would shout, 'Straggler!' and you would just shed them off—put them in another pen—and if you knew the person who owned it, afterwards you phoned them up. We used to take all the stragglers off. Saves you a lot of bother. But if they still didn't know who owned the straggler, they would auction it later on at the fank.

Then there were the ear-marks, lug-marks. Oh yes, on one farm I used to do an *eal stob* on the right and a *nip* on left[25]. Some people call that a *fork* on the right, instead of an *eal stob* but it's always an *eal stob* when you get it in the book. Now there's another great lug mark that they call a *back-half* or a *fore-half*. Or sometimes they could have a *double nip*. There is another one that isn't so very popular,

25   The Skye shepherds referred to the 'nip' as a beum.

which is a *slip*—you can have two forks, one in each ear, anyway. Some of the marks they had in the old days would have 3 nips out of the top of the ear on the left and 3 on the right. They still do it, like, the ones up the road there, they do 6 nips on the ear, very small ones—they watch what they do. And you sometimes see just the hole in the lug and that can be done with a punch, like a leather punch. In our day it was always just a penknife we used, but you can get tools now for it—oh aye, you can get them for the *back-half*, for the *fork*, for the *nip* and they can be used the same way.

Every year they used to sell all the sheep in Perth. When I started in Balquhidder, we took the sheep over the hill, *Beinn Sithean,* and I used to be sent away with the sheep over the hill to a field just above the station at Strathyre. And they were taken to the waggons there—that all the time I was there, until 1945. I think it was lorries after that, big two storey lorries, and nowadays it's three.

Then there was the dipping every year—in some places now, inoculation is all they use. But used to have to dip them twice a year. The police had to be told—they used to come and look at the strength of your dip too—well that was what it was supposed to be, but that never happened! Half the police that came to my father's farm it was more this they were after—Slainte! But if the police at that time had taken samples of the dip, there would have been an awful lot that would have been prosecuted—not too strong, but too weak! You know at one time, now I've never used it in all my years amongst sheep, but at one time, they used to dip the sheep with very, very good dip, and in the tank went whale oil, this was to keep the water off the sheep in the winter. Aye, it was waterproof. We never used it, but it was used. In my day I used to dip all the sheep in this district—Locherlour and up Glen Turret, that was me. Bare hands, mostly but of course no matter what cover you have on your hands the water still got up. And I've seen my arm here just red, and getting itchy, but that moves away as time goes on, but it was burn—I maintain that that's where I got this itch to start off with. It was burn. And in those days, we didn't wear spectacles or goggles or anything, and I'm telling you, if you got a splash of that dip in your eye, you weren't right for a wee while. It was so, so sore.

It used to be at one time, about ten pound of sliced dip, it had to be weighted down with hot water, stirring, stirring, stirring until all that stuff was melted—just like hot water with a dod o' butter, you know, it would melt. And out of that, you would do, say, 5 pounds of that stuff you would do 100 gallon. And when you put that into the tank, you could smell the sheep at least a fortnight after they were dipped! The Dieldrin was the thing that was in the dip at that time—Dieldrin[26], that is the word that was used, but they took away that and that finished it, the ticks got up like that. But now you see, they're no dipping the sheep, because of this. The dip nowadays, the likes of that, the dip they have nowadays, would be for 300 gallons of water, oh a wee cup, half a pint for 300 gallon—it was just like sour milk when you put it in a dipping tank, now that's no damn use! There's scab and the likes, and of course ticks is a different story altogether! Ticks can cause an awfu' damage an it's all caused by not using the proper dip and not proper heather burning.

The keepers nowadays don't burn heather at the right time of year—imagine burning heather in the October month! In our day it was always March and April and in Perthshire it was always the keepers. And if they're burning the heather properly, the young heather should be showing about a year and half afterwards. There is no use in heather being burnt unless it is like that, down flat, burnt right down.

Iain MacLean: It wasn't the keepers with us, in Skye, it was the children, the crofters' children. Always March and April, we youngsters used to do it. We'd get sent out in squads to

26   In the UK the use of dieldrin was banned in 1989.

burn the heather and we couldn't wait, we just loved it! And it was like tinder when we burnt it, every March and April, always before the birds started nesting. It would take off and bun right down to the ground, a big black patch, and that would be black till the next year it'd come up. You'd still have big areas of heather growing beside that patch, and then when that heather faded and dried out, you'd burn that patch the next year.

Jimmy: Nowadays they're burning heather and it stops at this height 'cause they are burning it at the wrong time of year! October! It's not ready for burning, not dry enough. And of course, the keepers nowadays have these quad-bikes. I was round an estate, where it has a main road through it, and it was all burnt nicely where it was being seen, and there were other bits that were just left, that should have been burned. They are burning the spaces that shouldnae be burnt, it should be the other side of the hill that they burn. Some o' them are burning the young heather, then stopping it. But nowadays what comes in its place, white grass, no' fit for sheep or nothing. That is what is happening. I was speaking to an old keeper the other day, he called in to see me, and he says, 'Look Jimmy, our days were hard, but we enjoyed it. Nowadays it's not hard at all. They don't even use a bloody brush! They've got cans of water on their back to put oot the fire.' No heather brush needed now. And now, look at all the ticks! Oh the boys who were here in my time—some o them were from Skye—by God, they knew how to burn the heather! It was maybe four or five acres at a time. When you've been amongst it all your days you could never forget. [27]

---

27   This conversation was recorded 9 October 2009, just a few weeks before Jimmy and his wife Mary moved from Locherlour, where he had worked for many years. Having lived in rural communities his whole life, he was anticipating the move to Crieff (to be nearer amenities if health should fail), so happened to drop by for a ceilidh while my cousin, Iain MacLean, was visiting. The reference to Skye is to our grandfather's croft in Glenconon, Uig. (MB)

2

Gaelic in Perthshire

Selina MacFarlane and Jean Hyndman
Comrie, 1999

> When we were young, people spoke Gaelic in the glens,
> Glenartney and Glen Lednock. And then there would be
> people coming in who would speak Gaelic and probably
> some of the villagers spoke Gaelic in those days.[28]

Though Gaelic was once spoken all over Perthshire, only a
few folk remember when it was the everyday speech of the
community. Although it lasted longest in the remote glens,
it was once so vibrant that Perthshire could boast some of
the finest bards in Scotland, such as Dugald Buchanan of
Balquhidder and Kinloch Rannoch and James MacGregor
from Comrie (and, later, Cape Breton). The current tendency
to 'blame outside forces' (or even the 'landed gentry') for the

---

28   Doris and I recorded Selina MacFarlane, Jean Hyndman and
her sister Eliza for our earlier project, *Remembered in Perthshire*, (1999).
Their reminiscences, covering a range of topics, are woven through
this collection as all three were interested in local history and tradition
and all had roots in Comrie. We are grateful to Hugh Hoffman the
following notes on genealogy: Selina Williamson MacFarlane, born 29
March 1915 at Glasdale, Comrie; Jean Hyndman (formerly known as
Jane) was born in 1921 in Scone; she died in 2008. Jean's sister Eliza
Hyndman was born in 1925, also in Scone, where their father worked
as an estate carter. Both parents were from the Mill of Ross, Comrie,
where they had a family home.

decline of the language gives entirely the wrong picture, as can be seen from the actual records of the time, which give a much more balanced view.

The Old Statistical Account of Scotland, Comrie, 1791-99

The common language of the people is Gaelic. All the natives understand it, but many, especially of the old, do not understand English well. All the young people can speak English; but, in order to acquire it, they need go to service in the Low Country. The Gaelic is not spoken in its purity, neither here nor in any of the bordering parishes…

The present incumbent [of the parish church, and writer of this report], Mr Hugh McDiarmed was admitted minister of Comrie in July 1781. The church is old, too small, and not in very good repair. There is another church 4 miles west from the village, in which divine service is performed, almost wholly in Gaelic, every fourth Sunday. The manse and offices were built in 1784. The glebe consists of near 9 acres, 6 of which are pretty good; the others are very poor. The stipend is, in money, 52l. 2s.3d; and, in grain, 16 bolls of meal, and 8 bolls of bear [sic, *bere*]; in all about 69l; and in this sum in included what is allowed for communion elements.[29]

Queen Victoria (1819—1901) was a young woman when she and husband Prince Albert first visited Scotland in August 1842. 'Albert and I were then only twenty-three, young and happy.' Thus began their love affair with Scotland, which was strongly influenced by their time spent in Perthshire. She kept a journal, the first of two[30], carefully describing what they saw and who they met, highlighting special moments as well as their personal interests. In those days, Gaelic was invariably the language of all the estate workers as well as that of the singers, musicians and dancers whose entertained them all over the Highlands.

---

29   OS, Vol XI, p.
30   The journal was later published as her book, *Leaves from the Journal of a Life in the Highlands, from 1848-1861.*

Queen Victoria, **Saturday, 10 September, 1842**
We walked to the dairy and back—a fine bright morning
… we drove with the whole party down to the lake,
where we embarked. Lady Breadalbane, the Duchess of
Sutherland, and Lady Elizabeth went by land, but all the
others went in boats. With us were Lord Breadalbane,
and the Duchess of Norfolk and Duchess of Buccleuch;
and two pipers sat on the bow and played very often…

Our row of 16 miles up *Loch Tay* to *Auchmore*, a cottage
of Lord Breadalbane's, near the end of the lake, was the
prettiest thing imaginable. We saw the splendid scenery to
such great advantage on both sides—*Ben Lawers*, with small
waterfalls descending its sides, amid other high mountains
wooded here and there; with *Kenmore* in the distance; the
view, looking back, as the loch winds, was most beautiful.
The boatmen sang two Gaelic boat-songs, very wild and
singular; the language so guttural, and yet so soft…[31]

The Queen was very attracted to the language and the culture,
though she was very much aware that English had become
the language of commerce as well as that of the upper classes.
Albert shared her enthusiasm and began to learn Gaelic. When
the Royal couple returned to Scotland two years later to spend
three weeks at Blair Castle, the Queen apparently expressed
her concern for the language. According to Dr John MacInnes
(friend and former colleague from the School of Scottish
Studies) there's a story from oral tradition that Queen Victoria
told the Sixth Duke and Duchess that, instead of English-
speaking nursemaids, they should employ Gaelic-speakers to
make sure that their children would speak the language of their
own people. Though this episode does not appear in either of
her journals, nevertheless it is borne out by the fact that the 7th
Duke, John Stewart Murray, (who was only two years old when
the Queen first visited) was, till the end of his days (1917), a
fluent Gaelic-speaker.

---

31   *Leaves from the Journal of Our Life in the Highlands*. London:
Smith, Elder, 1868, p. 45

The New Statistical Account of Scotland, 1844—45
The parish being situated on the borders of the Highlands
… we need not be surprised to find that Gaelic is spoken
in the back part of it, and the old Scotch dialect in the fore
part pronounced with the Gaelic tone and accent. There
are, however, very few persons in the whole parish who
do not speak or understand Gaelic. Most of the places are
evidently derived from that language…[32]

The English language is generally spoken, and has
gained ground greatly within the last forty years. At
present, scarcely a fourth part of the congregation attend
on the afternoon Gaelic service, whereas forty years
ago, the attendance on English was very limited. An
annual meeting for the encouragement and exhibition of
Highland games and dress was, some years ago, instituted
under high patronage in St Fillans…[33]

Queen Victoria, 30th August, 1849

After writing our letters, we set off on our ponies, with
Miss Dawson, MacDonald, Grat, Batterbury, and Hamis
[sic] Coutts; Hamis is Gaelic for James, and is pronounced
"Hamish." The road has been improved since last year,
and though it is still very rough, there are no fords to
pass nor real difficulties any longer. We rode the whole
way, and Albert only walked the last two miles. He took
a Gaelic lesson during our ride, asking Macdonald, who
speaks it with great purity, many words and making him
talk to Jemmie Coutts. Albert has already picked up many
words…

An announcement, 1878

Queen Victoria has appointed a Gaelic bardess, Mary
MacKellar, to translate into Gaelic her *Leaves from the
Journal of our Life in the Highlands*.[34] At the same meeting it

---

32   NS, p. 739—40
33   NS, p. 586
34   Glasgow University Special Collections has a copy of a Gaelic
Translation of Queen Victoria's *Leaves from the Journal of a Life in the
Highlands*, from 1848-1861, translated into Gaelic by the Rev. Mr. St.
Clair and also *More Leaves from the Journal of a Life in the Highlands from*

was announced that Queen Victoria is giving £200 towards the establishing of a Celtic chair in Edinburgh University.

There were several schools in Perthshire where Gaelic was taught, and the 7th Duke, whose children all spoke Gaelic, was keen that it should be the language of the whole area. He was particularly pleased that his youngest daughter, Evelyn (born in 1868), took a special interest in traditional stories and songs enjoyed among local people.[35]

Letter, from the 7th Duke of Atholl to his daughter Evelyn:

April, 1884

Dear, I can't say how pleased I am to see that you have an interest in the language. It is the one thing I have longed for all your lives, that you should all take a pleasure in learning the language of our forefathers, now alas fast passing away...[36]

As mostly all the estate workers were Gaelic speaking, this letter from the Duke, written when asked to consider a potential employee, reflect his commitment to Gaelic:

'Say to him I hope he will do all he can to learn Gaelic — I hate the idea of having a non-Gaelic speaking man.'[37]

In 1901, however, when a school inspector from the Scotch

1862 to 1882, in translation, *Tuilleadh dhuilleag bho m' leabhar-latha mu chunntas mo bheatha anns a' Ghaidhealtachd, bho 1862 gu 1882* (Edinburgh, 1886).

35 Lady Evelyn's poignant life-story is told in *Daughter of Atholl: Lady Evelyn Stewart Murray, 1868-1940* by Sylvia Robertson and Patricia Young, (Abertay Historical Society Publication), Dundee, 1996. 3rd edition, 2007, printed by, and available from, Blair Castle, Perthshire.

36 Thanks to Sylvia Robertson's research in the Atholl Archive the letters quoted here, as well as many interesting manuscripts from the Murrays of Atholl are now in print. See *Tales from Highland Perthshire*, p. 29

37 Op. cit., p. 28

Education Department visited the schools at Blair Atholl, Pitagowan and Stathtummel and found that Gaelic classes were being taught, he reported them to be a 'waste of time'. As a result, the Blair Atholl School Board was refused any support for the teaching of Gaelic or the employment of Gaelic-speaking teachers.

Letter from John Stewart Murray, Duke of Atholl, to the Scotch Education Department, 1901

Without entering into any discussion as to the circumstances of children in other districts, I am desirous of preserving the Gaelic Language in my own neighbourhood...'

Alas, however, it was to no avail, as the Education Department held their ground and children soon learned that Gaelic was not valued as part of their Scottish education. Meanwhile, the Murrays of Atholl set an example that demonstrated that children easily and naturally learn several languages, as their children learned to speak French and German as well as Gaelic and English. Lady Evelyn, meanwhile, developed a passion for Perthshire's vibrant oral tradition, becoming not only a fine Gaelic scholar but also a folklorist. To this day, her remarkable collection of Gaelic stories, songs and sayings testifies to the richness and strength of Perthshire Gaelic tradition.[38]

Mrs. Jean Innes
Balquhidder, 1990

Father always spoke Gaelic—all the shepherds spoke Gaelic, he conversed with them in Gaelic. I mean that was the language they used; they told him what was happening on the hill and what not. Yes, it was all Gaelic, Father's native language, and before I went to school I could

---

38 In 1958 the 10th Duke of Atholl, George Iain Murray, (1931—96) donated Lady Evelyn's collection of Gaelic tales to the School of Scottish Studies. Thanks to the careful work of Anthony Dilworth and Sylvia Robertson, part of this letter appears in their book, *Tales from Highland Perthshire, Collected by Lady Evelyn Stewart Murray,* (2009).

understand and speak it. But when I went to boarding school, you see, you'd to learn French, German… that was in Bridge of Allan at St Helen's School … I was five when I first went—it's very young, but there was nowhere else to go, you see, we couldn't go to the local school because there's no way of getting up and down—you couldn't drive every day, oh, you couldn't in those days.

Ella Walker
Killin, 1964

My father was a native of Ardeonaig and my mother of Glen Lyon, across the river from Invervar, and were they both Gaelic speakers. I was born in Glen Lochay, Old Duncroisk [1904]. The Walkers, father's people, originally came from somewhere down in the Borders—there's an old stone on the family grave, in the graveyard at Ardeonaig, the first date is 1767 I think, so it's quite old. Well they came up with a lot of other trades people—the then Lady Breadalbane brought them up—trying to civilize the Highlands after the Forty-five!

At home as a child, Gaelic was always spoken, oh yes, it was the language of the house. Everyone talked it in the house, we spoke it all the time but I'm afraid I got to a stage once I went to school, I *thought* in Gaelic and I was inclined to answer in English because I never went to school locally. The little school in Glen Lochay was two miles away and the Killin school was four miles away and I wasn't just awfully strong so I was sent to stay with my uncles and aunt in Callander and I spent all my schooldays in Callander. But I can tell you that when I was in Callander, all those years, I was the only child in a school of over 300 who could speak one word of Gaelic. And there was no Gaelic taught in school, none whatever, but the teachers used to try to get me to talk Gaelic but of course I was a bit shy and scared and they could hardly get a word out of me. I can remember several of them standing round me and trying "What's the Gaelic for this? What's the word for that?" I was terribly embarrassed.[39]

Selina MacFarlane and Jean Hyndman
Comrie 1999

Once the weavers were in, then English became more and more common, you know. It was always on the borders you know, Comrie it was always on the borders between the Highlands and the Lowlands.

Pat MacNab
Comrie, 2010

When I came to the glen I wasn't even five, I was only four— I was born on 5th December 1912 and we came to Comrie in 1916. The family were from Eigg, so it was all Gaelic—so at that age, I didn't speak a word of English. So, when I went to the school in Glenartney, they just came over me with the cane, a big long cane at that, and they made me speak English. Och, whack me! Mercy me, in my early days I had as much whacking, an' me with my kilt on, an' my backside black an' blue. Oh, yes, I wore the kilt all the time to school.

My brother Duncan was seven years younger than me, so he was born here—they were all born here, the rest of them, so it was English he had—he might have had the odd word, like myself nowadays. I grudge not knowin' it now. I can follow them in the singing there, I can follow that but for in a conversation, once I get a bitty excited it goes. In my young days, I didn't meet Perthshire Gaelic speakers, not a lot anyway, till I went to Killin—when I worked wi' the Robertsons at Muirlanich. John and the brother. Donald, they had Perthshire Gaelic and the old lady herself, they all had Gaelic. And the MacDiarmids, Loch Tayside, oh, they

---

39   Recorded by Dr Anne Ross, April 1964. School of Scottish Studies Archive SA1964/18

were bound to have Gaelic.

Then from Glen Lyon and a lot o these places, there were all these boys had plenty Gaelic in these days but you see that all that breed's growing out—there'll soon be nothing left o' my kind. They're all disappearing as regards to hill folk. And of course all the shepherds, everybody spoke Gaelic to the dogs:

Thig amach!
Thig air ais!
Thig a staigh!

Selina MacFarlane and Jean Hyndman
Comrie 1999

When we were young, there was an old lady in the village (Comrie) who had Gaelic, Mrs. MacNab. She was very elderly, and she was very correct. She was tall and always held herself very erect, very dignified, and she went to the Ladies' College in Edinburgh. She was sent there, which is quite extraordinary because her father was the gamekeeper, in Glen Lednock. But she went to the Ladies' College in Edinburgh so that she would be *properly* brought up, (like young ladies in Edinburgh, and of course she'd learn to 'speak properly'—in English, of course). And Gaelic was her mother tongue, but after her 'proper' education she always spoke English when we knew her. Her family went to the Gaelic services when she was a girl. At that time it was every Sunday, but then she said things changed, and the Gaelic services went into the afternoon, and then it just faded away because there were so few people left who spoke Gaelic.

Pat MacNab
Comrie, 2010

Mrs MacNab up in Glen Lednock? I remember her, she was there for years. No relation to me—I know fine where she was and she had the 'Heather Cottage'—it was before you'd go to the farm. And brother Duncan was at the farm just beside it there. And the two sisters they went down wi' their eggs in the washing basket. And Duncan was on a pushbike and he smacked right through them and all the eggs were smashed. And they were hurt an' all—he went smack into them, they were carrying the washing basket between them and they were in hospital and so was he.

Killin News: Killin and District Community Newspaper, **July, 1996**

Ella Walker who died on 30 June, age 92, was born at Easter Duncroisk, Glenlochay. Ella was a well known figure in Killin and was a great supporter of the Church and a keen Guildswoman. As an acknowledged Gaelic scholar, Ella was also keenly interested in local history... With her passing, a part of Killin's history has gone.

Pat MacNab
Comrie, 2010

Gaelic today? Well, there's Chrissie, but she's from Uist. Here? Comrie? No, I don't know a soul.

The New Statistical Account of Scotland, **Killin, 1845**

In the manse of Killin the present version of the Gaelic Scripture was begun. The Gaelic Testament was executed by James Stewart, from whom his son, the well-known Dr Stewart of Luss, obtained that knowledge and taste for Gaelic lierature which enabled him so faithfully to finish the Gaelic translations of the Bible. Killin may then fairly lay claim to the honour of this great work. [40]

Balquhidder & Killin, June, 1997:

The Rev. John Lincoln has been appointed to the parish of Balquhidder and Killin. He is a Gaelic speaker and, having learned the language in adulthood, is committed to keeping

---

40   NS. p.1087

the tradition of the area, once entirely Gaelic-speaking. There will be a bi-lingual service at Balquhidder Kirk in August to commemorate St. Angus's Day, when the prayers will be read by Mrs. Peigi Bennett who lives in Balquhidder.

The New Statistical Account of Scotland, 1844—45
In the manse of Killin the present version of the Gaelic Scripture was begun. The Gaelic Testament was executed by James Stewart, from whom his son, the well-known Dr Stewart of Luss, obtained that knowledge and taste for Gaelic literature which enabled him so faithfully to finish the Gaelic translations of the Bible. Killin may then fairly lay claim to the honour of this great work.

The Scottish Bible Society, Edinburgh, 2010
Bible Society launches new Gaelic Gospel, October, 2010. At the Royal National Mod in Thurso, the Scottish Bible Society launched a fresh translation of John's Gospel … aimed at younger Gaelic speakers and other readers who may have difficulty understanding the Bible. Dr Paul Ellingworth said, 'We are aiming to express John's original Greek text as accurately as possible, using words and idioms normally used by Gaelic speakers.'
Perthshire minister, the Rev John Lincoln of the Church of Scotland, Killin, is one of the team of five Gaelic translators who will continue to work on this new Gaelic translation of the Bible.[41]

---

41   From the Scottish Bible Society news, online. The other team members are the Very Rev John Angus Macdonald, Roman Catholic, formerly of Newtonmore, the Rev Ruairidh Maclean, Free Church of Scotland, Harris, the Rev John Urquhart, Church of Scotland, Skye and the Rev Dr Paul Ellingworth, former United Bible Societies translation consultant, Aberdeen.

3

EARTHQUAKES AND OTHER EXTRAORDINARY PHENOMENA

Selina MacFarlane, Jean and Eliza Hyndman
Comrie, 1999

There used to be a lot of earthquakes in Comrie at one time. Earthquake village! Oh it's a number of years since we really had a big one. The worst I remember was in 1947 and half the summer visitors went home. They thought the place was going to disappear.

The Highland fault line, that goes under this house [Drumearn House]. There was a lot of fear at one time as the houses would shake and you would feel tremors. That's why there's so many cracks in the walls ... but we don't really have [any major tremors], well maybe a few dishes rattle on the shelves. They really were bad years ago, things fell off the shelves in 1947 — I think was the last bad one. They used to pray in the churches... 1879, I think it was, they went into the church — 1869 they thought it was really serious.

Statistical Account of Scotland, Vol. XI, 1791
The Parish of Comrie: Earthquakes — This parish, and the neighbourhood, have, for more than 3 years past, been not a little alarmed by several sharp shocks of an earthquake. It was first felt, or rather loud noises, unaccompanied with any concussion, were heard by the inhabitants of Glenlednaig, during autumn 1789. These noises were first supposed to be peals of thunder; afterwards, as they were

heard sometimes when the sky was quite clear, the people imagined they were occasioned by the firing of carronades at Dunira. Finding, however, on inquiry, that they did not proceed from this cause, they were at a loss how to account for them, till the 5th of November 1789, when, about 6 o'clock in the evening, they were alarmed by a loud rumbling noise, accompanied with a severe shock of an earthquake. This shock, which is generally supposed to be the most violent of any that has happened here, was very sensibly felt over a tract of country of more than 20 miles in extent. Since that period the shocks have been very frequent, and at times pretty violent; but hitherto they have done no harm. Within these 3 or 4 weeks, since the weather has settled into drought, they have ceased altogether. The centre of the earthquake is, as nearly as can be guessed, about the mouth of Glenlednaig a mile or two north from the village of Comrie. What supports this conjecture is, that the people who live on the E. side of the glen, feel the earthquake begin in the N.W. and proceed in a south-easterly direction. Those who inhabit the country on the W. side of it, think that it takes its rise in the N.E. and expires in the W.

Perthshire Courier 7th **November 1839**
Earthquakes at Comrie
The following journalised record of the recent earthquakes has been forwarded to us by a respectable correspondent at Comrie.

Friday 4th October—One slight shock at half past four am. Noise but no tremor of the earth perceptible. State of weather not noted.
Tuesday 8th—One slight shock at half past five am Noise but no tremor perceptible.
State of weather not noted.
Thursday 10th—One severe shock at half past five am. This shock was much more severe than any felt for many years before. Great noise, and great tremor of the earth. Atmosphere moist; heavy rain in the evening, accompanied with violent winds.

Saturday 12th — In all ten shocks today. First about 1 pm; noise very loud; tremor of the earth very great. Atmosphere moist; the wind which had been somewhat high in the early part of the day, had sunk to a dead calm a little before the shock, but subsequently rose again; sky dark and lowering. Another shock took place shortly afterwards, accompanied by noise but no tremor. A third was felt about 3 pm. This was more severe than the first, and in some respects dissimilar. Its approach was not so sudden having given warning for about two seconds by a hollow murmuring sound. The noise was not only very great, but as if repeated, the redoubled report of a blasted rock. The tremulous motion of the earth was much more perceptible. Atmosphere moist ; wind as before, rising after the shock, yet not so much as to effect in any degree, the progress of the clouds. The heavens, more especially to the north and northwest, appeared as hung with sackcloth. A dense dark indescribable form of mist invested the mountains, whose broken crags here and there frowning through in awful majesty, gave to the scene an appearance ineffably grand, and in many respects terrible. Fourth, fifth, sixth seventh and eighth shocks, shocks at brief intervals, noise but no tremor. Ninth about 4 pm almost in every respect similar to the first. Tenth after a brief interval; noise but no tremor. During the first, third and ninth of these shocks, slates fell from houses, stones from walls, and furniture much moved.

Sabbath 13th — Three slight shocks, some say more, but no tremor. Weather not noted.

Monday 14th — One very severe shock at half past two pm, similar in almost every respect to the third shock of Saturday. Atmosphere moist; slight rain falling; sky dark and lowering; hills almost free of mist. This was succeeded by several slight shocks , but no tremor.

Wednesday 16th — A very severe shock at a quarter to three am. Noise very great, and tremor alarming. This shock was probably more severe than any of the former. Furniture much moved; in some houses the bells rang. Atmosphere moist; during the forenoon, no rain; heavy rain in the evening. Some slight shocks, but no tremor, excepting one

at half past five am similar to the first of Saturday.
From *Thursday17th till Tuesday 22nd*—some slight shocks
according to some accounts.
Wednesday 23rd—An indescribably dreadful shock at half
past ten pm. Compared with this, all which preceded it
are not to be named. The noise, which resembled that
of two or three shocks in close succession, was as the
noise of many thunders. The tremor of the earth was
dreadful. Atmosphere very heavy. Rain which had been
falling during the day descending in torrents, causing the
River Earn to be very much flooded. During this shock
chimney cans were thrown down and bricks from old
chimneys. In the neighbourhood portions of dry stone
and some walls rent. As might be expected the villagers
were alarmed, and became increasingly so; at 11 o'clock
when another shock, but by no means so severe as the
preceding one was felt. Shortly after this the Rev. Mr
Walker having made his appearance in the village was
requested by many who were now crowding the streets
to retire with them to the Secession Church, which he
did about 12 o'clock at night. The house was partly dark
and partly light. Nearly 300 people might be collected;
many of these were already seated, many more of them
however, keeping near the door as if afraid to enter.
After some entreaty, the most of them came in and sat
down. Mr W after a few words commenced the services
by giving out part of the 91st Psalm, which, having been
sung, he engaged in prayer. After this he gave an address,
which, having been followed by prayer of an elder of the
established church, the meeting dispersed about 2 am.
There was little sleep in the village during the night, there
having been, according to some accounts, not fewer than
14 shocks before day light. Most of these were attended
by no perceptible tremor.
Thursday 24th—Some slight shocks; noise but no tremor.
A full meeting in the Established Church in the evening;
services conducted by the Rev. Mr Mackenzie.
Friday 25th—some light shocks; noise, but no tremor.
A full meeting in the Secession Church in the evening;
services conducted by the Rev. Mr Laurie of Gargunnock.

Sabbath 27th — Some slight shocks, noise but, no tremor.
Monday 28th — Three slight shocks; noise but no tremor.

Comrie Parish Church, November, 1839:

At the Gaelic service, **Salm XCI**
     An neach sin tha'n a thàmh gach uair
     An ionad uaighneach Dhé
     Fo sgàil an Uile-chumhachdaidh
     Buan-chòmhnidh ni gach ré.

Let us sing together these verses from Psalm 91, to the tune Kilmarnock:

  1. He that doth in the secret place
     Of the most High reside
     Under the shade of him that is
     Th'Almighty shall abide

  3. Assuredly he shall thee save,
     And give deliverance
     From subtile fowler's snare, and from
     The noisome pestilence.

  4. His feathers shall thee hide; thy trust
     Under his wings shall be:
     His faithfulness shall be a shield
     And buckler unto thee.

  5. Thou shalt not need to be afraid
     For terrors of the night;
     Nor for the arrow that doth fly
     By day while it is light;

  6. Nor for the pestilence, that walks
     In darkness secretly;
     Nor for destruction, that doth waste
     At noon-day openly
  10. No plague shall near thy dwelling come
     No ill shall thee befall;

For thee to keep in all thy ways
His angels charge he shall.

15. He'll call on me, I'll answer him;
I will be with him still
In trouble, to deliver him,
And honour him I will.

Perthshire Courier 5th November 1840
 Earthquake at Comrie:

A smart shock was felt here on the evening of the 26th at a quarter to seven o'clock. Reckoned the severest ever felt here, vis, the one on the 22nd October last year (which it will be recollected convulsed Scotland almost throughout). At 10 deg, this last one would stand on the same scale about 4 deg. The seismometers, or earthquake markers, were on this last occasion very sensibly affected. One of them—Mr Milne's vertical force one ranged 4 deg on its scale, which is about three fourth of an inch from its zero, or point of rest. Another—the dip instrumen—indicated the shock to have come upon it at an angle of 45 deg. to the horizon in the direction of W by N. so that if the hill of Cluan be, as is generally supposed to be the case, directly over the focus of these shocks, this would give a depth to it under that hill, within the bowels of the earth, of about two miles. The barometer and thermometer were not affected. The former stood at 29 inches and the other at 48 deg. Fahrenheit. The night was calm and misty—Scotch Mist, it might be called for it was accompanied with a gentle drizzle. This is now the third shock that has been sensibly felt within the current month.

Perthshire Courier 26th November 1840
Comrie:

No fewer than four—some say six—shocks of earthquake were observed here between half past two pm, yesterday and seven this morning- all however, of the gentler kind. consisting largely of sounds resembling those caused by distant artillery. Modified by that hum or half musical tone, which generally serves to distinguish these subterranean explosions from serial ones., even when otherwise most like them. The seismometers were not sensibly affected. Yesterday was mild and pleasant—some rain in the fore part and high wind throughout the night.

Perthshire Courier 28th January 1841
Earthquake at Comrie:
About midnight between the 7th and 8th inst, a shock was felt here—one of the slighter kind, but sufficient to be indicated by some of the instruments used for the purpose of marking these phenomena. This last, judging from the indication given, was more from the south than usual.

Perthshire Courier 25th March 1841
At 1 pm on Wednesday, Comrie had a smart undulating shock of earthquake. As far as could be guessed from former shocks, this one would be heard about fifteen to eighteen miles. There has been no shock so great since the 18th January 1840. The weather was dry, calm and cloudy, the noise was louder than any undulating shock that had been heard.

New Statistical Account of Scotland, 1845
Earthquake at Comrie:
This parish has acquired some notoriety from its earthquakes. These very remarkable phenomena have undoubtedly been felt here at intervals for nearly fifty years, but of late have been very feeble and rare. The writer of this felt one earthquake very distinctly, and has heard of several others during his incumbency. At and after the time of the last Statistical Account, the earthquakes were so frequent and violent, and accompanied with such loud noises, as to occasion great alarm,—especially one which occurred on a Sabbath, while the congregation was assembled. There has been no plausible theory of the causes of these local earthquakes; their centre seems to be about the round hill above Comrie; they have been felt at twenty miles distance, but their effects at no time have been serious. Probably there is some connection between

the earthquakes and the numerous extinct volcanoes in this neighbourhood.[42]

Jean and Eliza Hyndman
Comrie, 1999

Do you remember about 1970 there was a bad earthquake? Well, maybe it had moved further east by that time, because that happened, they were having a few round about Methven and into Perth and we were just having little ones, tremors.

And Glasgow had one as well, chimneys shooglin' and falling off—that's right, there's a fault under the Clyde. I was at Bearsden when one happened and they were running about wondering what this was. They eventually came and asked if I'd fallen out of bed! And being from *Comrie,* (which happens to be in the nation's capital of earthquakes), I asked them, 'Have you never heard of earthquakes?' That's the one that goes through from Renfrew under the Clyde.

Pat MacNab
Comrie 2010

I was on the top of a dyke in Glenartney at ten years old, and I was first hit by the shock of it—on the top of the dyke. I went back home and Mother's dishes, she had yon great big shelves, and the plates were all lying smashed on the floor. There was two earthquakes in my young day—I'll guarantee there was two, another when I was about thirteen or fourteen. I was on the way to school when the other one struck. I was in the kilt an' going over a fence, an' I got the wire between my legs and of course I didn't know what it was! And mother's dishes were knocked out that time as well. But anybody getting injured, not that I know of.

---

42   NS. Vol. XI p. 580—81

FLOODS AND FLASHING LIGHTS

Selina MacFarlane, Jean and Eliza Hyndman
Comrie, 1999

The Highland Brahan Seer forecast, he said we were going to disappear under water ... that it would be then, and they all went to the church to pray.

Aye, but if you think of the dam in Glen Lednock, part of which had to be rebuilt, there's lots and lots of escape routes for the water before it would affect Comrie, if you think of all the valleys between here and there. Then of course there's the three rivers in Comrie, that's what Comrie means, 'the meeting of the waters' The Lednock, the Ruchell and the Earn.

The people that live on the banks of the Earn are not really in much danger, that's the odd thing. We lived right on the Earn, at the mill up there, for forty years and we weren't in any danger. But since we moved, we're two fields away from the Ruchell, which is dangerous. It just comes down... But it's not a problem, it's the field next door to us that floods, pours into the garden. They're doing something to it, to shore up the banks, but that just diverts it to somebody else.

Perthshire Courier 26th **November 1840**
Comrie: Remarkable Phenomenon:
On Tuesday evening the 17th instant, between seven and eight o'clock, an interesting appearance was observed in the sky over this place. From a semi-circular small black cloud on the verge of the western horizon at the point N.W. by W. all the other clouds in view spun out into long dark streaks diverging like spokes from the nave of a wheel. After extending in almost unbroken lines over the whole sky, again converged in an exactly similar form on another small black semi-circular cloud, in the opposite point of the horizon. At each focus within the spokes the light of the aurora borealis was very distinct, leaving

no doubt as to the cause of this unusual arrangement of the clouds, and contrasting beautifully with the dark dresses of the present fleecy partners of these "merry dancers". The western focus was at first brilliant, and while it continued so the other was more faint.

The Auld Hoose, Gask,
sketched by **Lady Nairne**
A.K. Bell Library Collection

Pitfour House, Glencarse, c. 1900
Home to **Christian Murray**
"My room was right up there, top floor
with 52 steps…" (at the right-hand
corner).

Thatched houses, Killin, c. 1900

'The houses were all thatched
when I was a boy…'
—**Allan Walker**, 1964
A.K. Bell Library Collection

Pat MacNab, Glenartney, 1920s ' we were country born and bred, an' used to doin' a lot o' things about the glen an' all.
MacNab family Collection

Pat MacNab sits by the hingin lum in the longhouse, Muirlanich, 2001
'I went there in the spring o' twenty-eight…'
Margaret Bennett Collection

Mary Mathieson's grandmother, 'Granny Kennedy' with four of her twelve children, on the croft, Glen Ogle, 1888. Mary's father is seated in front.

'I was born in a croft in Glen Ogle just before the end o' the First World War, 1918… My father spoke Gaelic… his name was Donald Kennedy'
Mathieson family collection

Lochearnhead Hotel staff, early 1900s 'My mother was the dairymaid at the Lochearnhead Hotel…' **Mary Mathieson's mother** (front row far right)

Mary Mathieson, Lochearnhead, 1980s Family collection.

Jimmy Stewart (L) with Gregor MacGregor and Duncan Stewart, Balquhidder, 1945.
John McNaughton collection

Mary and Jimmy Stewart, c. 1950
'And I'll tak' ye tae Glen Isla near Bonnie Glenshee…'
Stewart collection

Jimmy and Mary Stewart, 2010
M. Bennett Collection

Jean Hunter, St. Fillans
Charles Hunter collection

Jean Innes, 'Jean the Braes',
Balquhidder, 1980s.
John McNaughton collection

The book + CD are available, price £10 from the A.K. Bell Library (Perth), Comrie Development Trust, Coda Music (Edinburgh), Amazon, Footstompin' and several bookshops.

You may also order by post from the publisher, Grace Note Publications
Please fill out your details and send a cheque payable to Grace Note Publications

NAME:..

ADDRESS:..

....

....

Number of books @ £10...

+ Post & package:
£2 for 1 book, £3 for 2 books, £4 for 3 or more...................

TOTAL ENCLOSED ....

Grace Note Publications
'Grange of Locherlour', Ochtertyre, by Crieff, Perthshire PH7 4HS
Tel. 01764 655 979   Email: gonzalo@gracenotereading.co.uk

Queen Victoria's visit,
Loch Tay, 1842,
'two pipers sat on the bow…'
A.K. Bell Library Collection

A piper plays for passengers on the
'Queen of Lochearn', 1920s
Jean Hunter recalls , 'there used to be
what they called 'the Bathing Parade' …
and you just got in the boat and got
across to the other side.'
Ewan Cameron Collection

The Earthquake House, Comrie, 2010
Grace Note Publications Collection

Comrie. Aberuchill Castle.

Aberuchill Castle
A.K. Bell Library Collection

The Scotsman - Thursday, 5th February 1914, page 7
You searched for: aberuchill castle

ABERUCHILL CASTLE

SERVANTS' NARROW ESCAPE.

The first discovery was made at Aberuchill Castle, where the only occupants were five domestic servants. One of them awakened about 4.30 and discovered that her bedroom was full of smoke. She at once roused the other four servants, and they all with difficulty made their way downstairs, where the drawingroom furniture was seen to be ablaze, having apparently been saturated with paraffin or some other inflammable liquid. The castle belongs to Mr G. C. L. Dewhurst, and is usually occupied by his mother (Mrs Jones), but that lady had lately been residing with her mother at Craggish, Comrie. The servants at once proceeded to the estate offices, about fifty yards away, and roused the workmen who lost no time in getting the castle fire appliances put into action. With an abundant supply of water to aid them, the men succeeded in confining the fire to the drawing-room, and they were greatly aided in their efforts by the resistance offered by the "fog" already referred to, and by the fact that the wall between the drawing-room and the main part of the castle, being the original outer wall of the building, is three feet thick.

OLD PAINTINGS DESTROYED.

All the furniture and furnishings in the drawing-room were destroyed, including a new grand piano and a number of valuable old paintings, as well as the furnishings in several of the bedrooms where the servants had been sleeping.

...and white walls of the castle make

The suffragettes were regularly featured in the newspapers of the day with wide coverage for the Perth prison episodes.

Dr Walter Yellowlees with Elaine Harker, Aberfeldy, 2009
Gonzalo Mazzei Collection

Perthshire hill-folk at the fank on shearing day, (unidentified), 1950s
A.K. Bell Library Collection

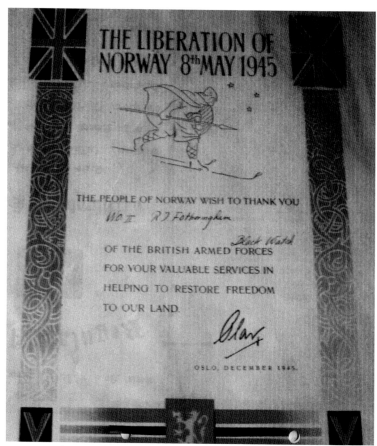

Military service documents from **Robert Fotheringham** who enlisted in the Black Watch in 1919 and was involved with the Liberation of Norway in 1945. These were among several papers shown by his 8 year-old great-grandson, **Dylan,** at Errol Primary School in 2010.

4

SCHOOLDAYS AND CHILDHOOD PASTIMES

OOR WEE SCHOOL...

The Old Statistical Account of Scotland, **Killin, 1792**
The parish schoolmaster here has a salary of 10 £ Sterling from the heritors, which, with school dues, and some perquisites as session-clerk, makes his living a little better than 20 £ Sterling annually. He has also a house and garden, and has ordinarily about 70 scholars, several of whom learn Latin, Greek, and French with him. There are 3 other schoolmasters in the parish, who teach only the reading of English and Gaelic, with writing and arithmetic; and 3 schoolmistresses, for teaching sewing and knitting of stockings...

The New Statistical Account of Scotland Comrie, 1845
The Rev. William MacKenzie: All parents show a laudable desire to educate their children ... in 1836 there were seven schools in this parish... Besides the common branches taught in all schools, the Parish teacher instructs in Greek, French and mathematics... The fees in all schools are, per quarter, 2s. for English; 2s. 6d. for English and writing; 3 s. for English, writing, and arithmetic; and 5 s. for Latin, inclusive of every other branch. There are none between six and fifteen years of age who cannot read or write; and, as far as is known, there are no natives of this parish above fifteen years of age who cannot read and write... There is a parochial library in Comrie containing about

500 volumes. It was commenced in 1822… There is also a small subscription library at St. Fillans; and a small circulating library at Comrie…[43]

Kirstie Pretious, Age 9
Errol, 2010

My gran told me that she went to a small village school at the age of four. There were four different age ranges in one classroom. Only one teacher in each room, she had to look after four classes. In my gran's class there was a lady teacher her name was Mrs McCabe. Every child had a slate and chalk on which they wrote a word and drew a picture. There was no central-heating and each room had a small stove. Turf (peat) was used to heat each room. The children were often frozen. At potato picking time her granddad would knock on the school window and ask if his three little helpers could be spared for a day's potato picking. My gran's name is Joan McConnell.

Christian Murray
Pitfour, Glencarse, 1920s and 30s[44]

We didn't go to school. My father didn't approve of girls going to school … we had a governess who lived in, poor thing. The domestics didn't approve of her so she was left very much alone. It must have been lonely for her—very, but one didn't realize it at the time. She must have been bored stiff—and with three horrible children to look after— three girls, then a long gap and then my brother arrived and he was very spoilt, or at least we thought he was spoilt. The Governess was Miss Reddy and she was very good that governess because she was interested in the things herself and was able to pass it on to us. We asked the questions and she gave us the answers. She was very knowledgeable,

---

43   NS, Vol. XI, pp. 590—93
44   Recorded 2010

interested in nature, names of the birds, wild berries and gardens and flowers.

We were always kept at it: 'Get on with your homework!' Not just five days a week, we were unlucky, *six* days a week! On the Saturdays we were made to do jobs in the garden or in the house. Yes, I can see that now—my sisters and I, it seemed to be forever!

Selina MacFarlane, Jean and Eliza Hyndman
Comrie, 1920s and 30s:

Jean: Remember we used to sing:

> Oor wee school's the best wee school
> It's made of stones and plaster;
> The only thing that's wrong with it
> Is the baldie-heided master.

But I don't think we were ever serious 'cause we wouldn't have been where we are if it hadn't been for the headmaster, Mr Murray.

Selina: Oh he was good, a good schoolmaster.

Eliza: He came on me one day standing in the corridor, 'cause I'd fallen out with Miss MacKenzie and he said 'What are you doing here?' And I said 'Oh, she got tired of me and put me out.'

So he said, 'Why was that?

I said, 'Well, that cupboard'—she had a cupboard with shelves and books—I said, 'I've read every one of those books and I'm tired of them.'

So he said, 'Well come with me,' and he took me to the bookcases and he gave me a book to read. I can't remember exactly what it was, a Dickens, and I enjoyed it. He encouraged me to read.

The New Statistical Account of Scotland, 1844—45
The girls in addition to the usual branches [of schooling]
are taught sewing and knitting...[45]

Jean, Eliza, and Selina
Comrie, 1999

We made the most unsuitable garments you could ever
imagine... of unbleached calico. I think we made a lap bag
first, then you made an apron or something. Then in the
'qualifying' [Primary 7] we made the most awful knickers
that you've ever seen. [Laughter] ... they had a
yoke like that at the front and they were gathered
onto the yoke. They had elastic, which Miss
Duncan measured below the knee. Oh, we never
met anyone who wore them —oh no! It was just a
waste of money.

Also in the sewing class we made a 'duchess
set' — there were three bits, one a longer one that
went in the middle of the dressing-table, and a smaller one
either side, which probably the powder would go on, and
something on the other side... You put a hem round it then
you took different colours to embroider them. The kind
of embroidery was just straight stitches and it had to be
matching. You went along the top, in out, in out in blue.
Then you went along the bottom of the hem, in out, in out,
in blue and then these stitches had to go exactly under each
other or you had to take them back. Then you put a cross
stitch in the spaces. And Jean got the strap every week in
life, either for cutting off the threads without finishing them
off, or talking. And then she got a prize at the end of the
year for sewing, which we thought was ridiculous!

And we had knitting. The first thing was a square, a pot-
holder Then socks—usually, ankle socks. And you learned
to turn a heel... You used to give it a pull and stretch it—oh
it was exciting, I can tell you, doing that! Then [in a later

---

45   NS, Vol. XI, p. 1093

class] we made a jumper.

Meanwhile, the boys got handwork. They made things with raffia and later, basketwork, and making models when they were in Primary seven... Oh life was exciting, I can tell you!'

Katie Louise Sinclair, age 10
Errol, 2010

My mum told me that her grandmother knitted a shawl that was so finely knitted my great grandmother could pass it through her wedding ring. She then passed it on to my granny who did the same and passed it through her wedding ring. My granny then gave that to my mum who has already passed it through her wedding ring and will give it to me when I have my first child. My Mum's name is Joanne Sinclair.

Jean Hyndman
Comrie, 2001

For gym classes, in our day you had to take off your gym-slip and your pink jersey, about this colour. (I happen to be wearing a pink jersey today!) This is the only time I've ever had one this colour since! And put on quite large knickers—they were greeny, not as dark as bottle green, a Greek dress with just a plain top and the waist was caught, and you'd a band round the middle and slits up the side, so you could move... And every 'Warship Week' or 'Victory Week' or whatever they were raising funds for, we had to go the park or the hall, whatever time of the year it was and do marching and counting in those blessed things.

IN THE PLAYGROUND

Jean and Eliza

In Comrie a favourite game was 'Who's afraid of the big bad wolf?' We stood in groups facing and somebody would be the big bad wolf and I don't remember what the trigger was. Sometimes you were quite free to run forward and other times it wasn't safe.

The boys preferred games like football... and they used to play games like cowboys and Indians—they'd to go 'Bang-bang you're dead!' Then count to fifty and your alive again... then they joined in the game again. That was our generation!

Selina

We played Peevers—we played it along the pavement... oh probably with our mothers' dressmaking chalk!

Balquhidder Primary School playground, 1985:
The children are Alquinn, Berta, Caroline, Christopher, Cisca, Fraser, Jennifer, Johann, Kelly, Lucy, Nicola, Peter and Sean.

We play hopscotch[46]—you have this sort of square and it's up to one to ten, and you get a stone and you throw it on number one, and you're not allowed to stand on the number with the stone so you have to go onto two, six and four, you have to put two feet on and all the other numbers you have to hop on, and there's a line around each number so if you step out of the box you're out so once you get round to ten you choose one of the numbers, and you're allowed to do what you want on it.

MB: Is there a special time of year you usually play that one?

---

46   In most areas of Scotland the term is 'peevers' or 'peever beds', 'hopscotch' being the English term for the game.

Children: The spring.

'Pipey'

You get a football, and you need a good flat wall which isn't on a slope and you've got to have two people and it's something like squash—you have to kick the ball against the wall and then the other person's got to run up, and the ball's got to touch the wall, and if the other person doesn't get the ball before it stops then he's out! Well, this game is called Pipey and we usually play this in the spring.

'Conkers'

And in the autumn we play conkers[47]—you go and get a horse-chestnut and you make a hole through it and you have to go and put a string through the middle and other people have to do that too. Then you have to go and you stand facing each other. And one person holds out his conker on the string and you have to try to smash their conker with your one. And the one who smashes the first conker is the winner.

'Kiss, cuddle and torture'

Well its boys against girls, and the girls have to catch the boys and then they get them against the wall and say, 'kiss, cuddle or torture?' And they have to choose.

MB: And what do they usually choose?

Boys: Torture!

MB: Is that the best of the three, kiss, cuddle or torture?

Girl: Well it depends which girl it is.

Boy: Torture is a kick up the bum.

Girl: It isn't always—it's any kind of torture.

Boy: Well torture is sometimes a kiss and a cuddle depending on who it is! And it depends what the rules are and how we're playing it. If it's torture and it's kiss and cuddle, it depends which girl it is. You decide when you see.

---

47   Health and Safety rules now forbid the game in school playgrounds.

'The Tickling Game'

Well usually there's one or two people 'It', or every man for himself. And you've got to catch people and tickle them and if you get tickling and you find a really tickly person then you call all the others and you all pile on top and tickle them.

'Farmer, Farmer'

You have a farmer and they stand at one end of the playground. Then you have quite a lot of people standing at the other end of the playground from them and then we say, 'Farmer farmer may we cross your golden river?' and the farmer says, 'Only if you've got the colour,' and they might say blue, and if you've got blue on you run to the farmer and the first person to reach the farmer becomes the farmer.

'British Bulldogs'

You part up, say girls against boys and we get teams and one person is 'It' and they say, 'Lucy, shall we try and run to the rest?' And if we got there, she would say 'British Bulldogs!' and we would all run, But if I caught her, Lucy and I would link up and try and catch all the rest.

MB: Where would you play that?

Child: Up on the grass there. You wouldn't play it on a hard surface like this because it's too dangerous.

'The Dragging Game'

We play one called the 'dragging game' which is a bit rougher than British bulldogs. You get two teams usually girls against boys and we usually go on that hill there, and you get one base at the top of the hill and one base at the bottom of the hill and your teams stay in those. The idea is to rush out and capture all the other team, and you can run in but if you enter the other person's space then you're caught. And you can be freed—people can drag you into the base, and you can be freed if somebody pulls you out by the hand. The idea is just to drag all the other people into your base—then that team wins.

MB: Where did you learn that one?

Children: We made it up.

'The Ragman'

You have a mother and you have some children as rags and you have a ragman. And the ragman comes and asks for some rags, so the mother sends away eh some of the rags and the ragman tells the rags things to say to the mother. And if they're nice things then she gives them a cake and if they're not nice things she chases after them with a stick.

'Coloured Eggs'

You have a wolf, and a mother and lots of people as eggs and all the eggs are given a colour. And the wolf comes up and asks the mother for some eggs. So the mother says 'what colour?' So he asks for a colour, and if he shouts out your colour you've got to run to his den and back without being caught and if you get caught you're the wolf.

'Dodge Ball'

You get a football and everybody spreads out and the person with the ball has to try and hit the people on the legs. And if you get hit by the ball you have to try and hit the people, and you're not allowed to run with the ball.

Games of Tig

We play *tunnel tig*. Well there's a person that's 'It' and he has to catch them and when he's caught them they have to stand with their legs wide and they have to wait for someone else to crawl under and make them free and if you're caught three times then your 'It'

And there's another game called *hospital tig* where, say someone was hit and they got you on the shoulder then you would hold your shoulder—because that's sort of an injured part, and you run like that, holding your shoulder. And if you get tigged again, then you're 'It'.

There's another game called *aeroplane tig*. We all play and then there's one that's 'It' chasing us. And if you get caught you've got to hold your arms out like that and if someone runs under your arms then you're free.

And there's **high tig.** Somebody's 'It' and they've got to try and catch you but they can't catch you if you're on a high bit, like a dustbin or on the top of that little wall and if you're caught then your 'It'.

We also play *chain tig.* Well there's one person 'It' and if they catch someone then they've got to hold hands or link up and they've got to run about together, make a chain and catch everyone. And when everyone's caught the last person that was caught is 'It' again.

Choosing 'It' and Counting Out

Eliza, Jean and Selina
Comrie 1999

In our day, (1920s and 30s) we'd have those rhymes for choosing 'It':

> Eenie, meenie, minie, mo
> Catch a tiger by the toe
> If he bites let him go
> Eenie meenie minie, mo.
>
> One potato, two potato,
> Three potato four
> Five potato, six potato,
> Seven potato more
>
> Out goes she!
> Eetle, ottle, black bottle
> Eetle ottle, out

If you want a piece and jam
Please step out.

And we would do that over and over again till each person
went out and there was only one left — she was 'It'.

Skipping Rope Rhymes and Songs

Playtime at Balquhidder Primary School, 1985

This is a skipping game. You have one person at each end to
turn the rope and you have the person in the middle. And
you have to pick a name for them, a boy's name, and that
means it's the one they're going to marry. And if they land
on a 'Yes 'at the end, that means they *will* marry them and if
they land on a 'No' they won't.

All the girls in London lived a happy life,
Except for Lucy who wants to be a wife,
A wife she shall be and hunting she shall go
Along with Robert E-I-O.
He kissed her and he cuddled her
And sat her on his knee
And said dear Lucy 'Will you marry me?'
'I'll marry you if you'll marry me
On the first day of September.'
Yes!

'Helicopter'

Well you get a short rope, about that short (a one-person
skipping-rope) and you tie a weight on the end and you get
about 4 players and one of them stands in the middle and
swings the rope round and round and the others chant this
song, and it gets lower and lower and you have to try and
jump the rope as many times as you can and if you trip the
rope then you have to go in the middle.

All chant:

> Helicopter, helicopter, please come down,
> If you don't I'll break your crown.

Now she's caught in the helicopter blade so she goes in the middle!

'I like coffee, I like tea'

This one's called 'I like coffee, I like tea. You have a skipping rope and a person doing the skipping says 'I like coffee I like tea,' and then they say a person they like 'in with me' and then that person has to jump in and they have to see how many times they can jump together.

> I like coffee, I like tea,
> I like Lucy in with me,
> 1, 2, 3, 4, 5, 6, 7, 8, 9!

'Salt, pepper, vinegar,'

And you can go like that, one on each end of the rope and you jump in and do—'Salt, pepper, vinegar,' go faster and faster and faster.

> Salt, pepper, vinegar, mustard!
> Salt, vinegar, mustard, pepper!
> Salt, vinegar, mustard, pepper!
> Salt—Who's next?

'Keep the Kettle Boiling'

This is a skipping game, and you start by getting a really long skipping rope and then there's two people at each side, one on each end of the rope. And the first person jumps in and it goes:

> Keep the kettle boiling, pour it through the spout,
> Keep the kettle boiling then jump out,'

And you keep the rope spinning and then the person jumps out and then another person jumps in while the ropes still going. And everybody can have a turn.

> Keep the kettle boiling, pour it through the spout,
> Keep the kettle boiling you are out!

And you can sing the song about the teapot and at the same time you can do actions for a teapot.

All chant:
> I'm a little teapot short and stout,
> Here's my handle, here's my spout.
> When the waters boiling hear me SHOUT!
> Tip me up and pour me out.

MB: Can you show me the actions again for 'I'm a little teapot'?

Children demonstrate:

> short—crouch down,
> stout—hands spread to indicate girth
> here's my handle—bend one arm, hold hand on hip
> here's my spout—hold the other arm, elbow bent
> upwards and wrist bent out
> when the kettles boiling—twirl your arms around
> hear me SHOUT! (just shout!)
> Tip me over and pour me out—bend over on one leg.

And you have two people turning the rope and the person skipping does the actions in the middle as the rope turns.

HAND-CLAPPING GAMES

You face each other and then clap and do the rhyme, singing:

When Susie was a baby, a baby Susie was,
She went a goo goo a goo goo goo.
When Susie was a toddler, a toddler Susie was,
She went a mum, mum a mum, mum, mum.
When Susie was a schoolgirl, a schoolgirl Susie was,
She went a miss, miss,
I got my knickers in a terrible twist!
When Susie was a teenager a teenager Susie was,
She went an ooh! Ah! ooh! Ah!
I left my knickers in my boyfriend's car!
When Susie was a mother, a mother Susie was,
She went a Ssh! Ssh! A ssh, ssh ssh!
When Susie was a granny a granny Susie was,
She went a knit, knit a knit, knit knit!
When Susie was a ghost a ghost Susie was
She went ah-oooooooh!

BALL BOUNCING

Jean, Eliza, and Selina
Comrie

Then, if anyone had a rubber ball, that was great! (singing):

> One, two, three a leerie
> Four, five, six a leerie
> Seven, eight nine a-leerie
> Ten a leerie overball.
>
> One, two, three a leerie
> I saw Mrs Peerie
> Sitting on her bumbaleerie
> Eating chocolate biscuits.

Playing with Words

Mary Taylor,
school-teacher in Comrie, 1930s

And you had songs and rhymes and riddles:

    Come-a-riddle, come-a riddle,
    Come a rot-tot-tot
    A wee, wee man in a red, red coat;
    A staff in his hand
    and a stane in his throat
    Come-a-riddle, come-a riddle,
    Come a rot-tot-tot   *—a cherry*

    If a herring and a half cost three bawbies,
    how much would you get for elevenpence?
                         —eleven

I was born in Auchterarder in 1908. People used to say:

    Auchterarder lang an sma;
    Dirty doors and weavers a'.

And you'd sing:

    One, two three, four five,
    I caught a fish alive
    Six seven, eight, nine, ten
    Then I let it go again.

    Why did you let it go?
    Because it bit my finger so—
    Which finger did it bite?
    This little finger on the right.

Balquhidder Primary School, 1985

Child: Knock, knock
MB: Who's there?
Child: Donut.
MB: Donut who?
Child: [singing] Do-not forsake me, oh my darling!

Child: Knock, knock
MB: Who's there?
Child: Gorilla.
MB: Gorilla who?
Child: G'rilla me-a hamburger! [in mock-accent]

Child: Knock, knock
MB: Who's there?
Child: Lettuce.
MB: Lettuce who?
Child: Lettuce me in!

MB: We used to sing, 'Let us with a gladsome mind…'

Child: Knock, knock
MB: Who's there?
Child: A wee boy who's too small to reach the doorbell!

Child: Knock, knock
MB: Who's there?
Child: Doctor.
MB: Doctor who?
Child: Oh how did you guess!

Child: Knock, knock
MB: Who's there?
Child: Isobel.
MB: Isabel who?
Child: Is a bell necessary on a bike?

Child: Knock, knock
MB: Who's there?
Child: Nobel.
MB: Nobel who?
Child: No bell, that's why I knocked!

Child: Knock, knock
MB: Who's there?
Child: Police.
MB: Police who?
Child: P-lease let me out!

Child: Knock, knock
MB: Who's there?
Child: Irish.
MB: Irish who?
Child: I-arrest-you in the name of the law! [pronounced like 'Irish stew']

Child: Right, what do you call a man with a car on his head?
MB: I don't know — what do you call a man with a car on his head?
Child: Jack! What do you call a man that's been buried for six years? Pete! And what do you call a man with three rabbits up his bum?
MB: Oh gosh, I don't know!
Child: Warren!

PARTY GAMES

Selina, Jean and Eliza, in the 1920s and 30s

We sang 'The farmer's in his den' ...We all walked round in a circle and the farmer was in the middle.

The farmer's in his den,
The farmer's in his den,
Hey-ho, ma daddy-o
The farmer's in his den.

The farmer wants a wife....[etc]

The wife wants a child....

The child wants a nurse

The nurse wants a dog...

The dog wants a bone...

The bone won't break...

And we'd sing this last verse louder and faster and batter the poor bone! We used to play that at parties.

Balquhidder, 1985:

At parties we play **'Ring a ring o' rosies'**, **'Pass the parcel'**, **'Postman's Knock'** and **'Chinese Whispers'.** For Chinese Whispers you make a circle and you think of a word or words and then you pass it on to the next one, you whisper it in their ear. And then everybody in the circle does that until it gets right round to where it started. At the finish of it there could be different words. And we have an action song called Father Abraham—Mrs Mann (head teacher) taught us:

Children sing:

Father Abraham, has many sons,
many sons had father   Abraham,
I am one of them, and so are you
so let's all praise the Lord,
    Right hand.

Father Abraham, has many sons,
many sons had father Abraham,
I am one of them, and so are you
so let's all praise the Lord,
   Right hand, Left hand.

Father Abraham, has many sons,
many sons had father Abraham,
I am one of them, and so are you
so let's all praise the Lord,
   Right hand, Left hand, Right foot.

Father Abraham, has many sons,
many sons had father Abraham,
I am one of them, and so are you
so let's all praise the Lord,
   Right hand, left Hand, right foot, left foot.

Father Abraham, has many sons,
many sons had father Abraham,
I am one of them, and so are you
so let's all praise the Lord,
   Right hand, left Hand, right foot, left foot, Nod your
   head.

Father Abraham, has many sons,
many sons had father Abraham,
I am one of them, and so are you
so let's all praise the Lord,
   Right hand, left Hand, right foot, left foot, nod your
   head and turn around.

Father Abraham, has many sons,
many sons had father Abraham,
I am one of them, and so are you
so let's all praise the Lord,
   Right hand, left Hand, right foot, left foot, nod your
   head and turn around, sit down!

Christian Murray,
Comrie, 2010 — Glencarse, 1920s

At Pitfour, we could play hide and seek in the house—
down in the scullery and up to my bedroom—that's it in
the picture, on the top floor. And on the lawn we played
rounders, with a bat or sometimes a tennis racquet, though I
don't think we knew anything about tennis. We'd play with
anyone who came in for tea or anything, the visitors, would
play with us—and my older sisters and they didn't approve
of me, they thought I was a bit rebellious! My little brother
didn't play, as he was much younger, a different generation
really, seven years younger than me.

And we were forever walking! We were walked every
day by the governess or nursery-maid, come rain or shine.
Nanny was just sitting there at home tapping her feet and
saying, "Get along, get along! Down the drive! Turn to
the left!" Just about every day we went on a long walk
that went on forever and ever, I thought I'd never get to
the end of it. But it didn't do us any harm. We had things
pointed out to us like birds and things. Our governess
was interested in teaching us something … wild flowers
… the names of some of them…snowdrops, aconites then
daffodils, my Father was very keen on having different
varieties.

Jean Hunter
St. Fillans, 2010

My mother's great-grandfather, I think, was the
schoolmaster up Glen Lyon but then came down to Perth.
Her father, our grandfather, who died in 1928, lived in
Crianlarich after he married, then after they had seven
children they came to live in Comrie, Cowden in Comrie.
But my dad worked in Perth—he was a solicitor—so our
home was in Perth they came to this area for their holidays.

My parents used to rent a house in St Fillans for the

month of August, then Mother and her sister bought Lake Cottage in 1931, for a holiday home. We used to go to St Fillans for two months of the year, July and August. And when we came for those two months, we came by train from Perth to St Fillans, but there was a lorry, the coal lorry was enlisted, hired to take all our gear, bicycles, luggage everything had to go on the coal lorry—Cummings the coal lorry would arrive. And every day, Dad commuted by train to his office in Perth. We used to go along the back lane to meet him off the train 6 o'clock train.

There used to be a boat plied up and down the Loch, it went from the Queens Pier over on the other side, across the loch, opposite St Fillans. You know where the War Memorial is in St Fillans? You cross the rustic bridge—that wooden bridge from the Drummond Arms and it's just there. Anyway there was a pier there from where the boat sailed—'The Queen of Loch Earn'—in the summer months up and down to Lochearnhead. And then it became un-seaworthy about 1939 so it never did it again. And there used to be what they called 'the Bathing Parade' at 12 o' clock and 5 o'clock, and you just got in the boat and got across to the other side. We used to go there, on this boat and you would be bathing—we nearly always went to this because it was a good safe place to swim. I was a bit younger than the rest of them but I would tag on and we'd swim. Feel the cold? I think we just were Spartan! If you were a child you went in and afterwards shivered on the bridge or the bank. I suppose there were probably days we didn't do it because it would be too miserable, but you don't really remember that.

I had knitted shorts my mother made, with a bib on it and it had silver buttons at the back, for the straps over. And I remember there was this thunderstorm one day. We were staying in Lake Cottage in St Fillans at the time and because it was a wet day we were playing cards in the sitting room. And I had my back to the window and of course my big cousins, boys, and my brother told me, 'Oh you'll be struck, you'll be struck by lightning you've got your metal buttons on!' I was scared stiff! My Mother had knitted it. It was sort like a play-suit, I suppose.

And you had the golf course—you could have fun— every day it was the golf course and picnics on the loch-side. And this friend of mine, she was a year older than me, you know we were five and six together and we used to go and play golf. Can you imagine? On the golf course at St Fillans, at the age of five! We did what was called the Inner Circle, in the morning because we were allowed—I suppose it took us about 20 strokes to get to the first tee, first green rather! I had a little bag for my clubs, well I suppose they were child's size. I remember the first driver. Well it wasn't a new one, but it was new to me.

In those days (1930s), what they charged was ten shillings[48] for a family membership for the year—and there were five of us—then you could play as often as you liked. Well we played in the mornings so we weren't really in the way of most of the more serious golfers. But I was never good, I didn't play, I used to play *at* golf rather than play golf. One of my uncles who came in August, he was really keen. My Mother was quite good actually and they played regularly, they played 18 holes—they would play golf in the morning and then picnic in the afternoon and then the serious ones would have another game of golf in the evening, early evening. And you picked up the vocabulary and everything and it's quite funny because I haven't played since I have gone south at all and you know the people there are sort of new to golf by my standards. So if I come out with, sort of 'golf terminology, it's 'How do you know about that?'

I just say, 'Well living in Scotland it's part of your life in a way.'

---

48   In modern currency, 50 pence.

Mary Mathieson
Lochearnhead, 2010—Glenogle, 1920s

When we were young we used to play wee houses in
Glenogle. Sometimes we had the larder for a wee house.
We'd just get bits of broken dish and things like that, and
wash them—bits you'd find when you they're ploughing,
you would collect them, wee treasures and wash and clean
them, like a wee set of dishes. Sometimes you'd get a cup
with the handle, but maybe it was cracked, that was great.
Mairi next door would tell you, she was the same. We'd play
for hours wi' just rubbish—other folks rubbish. Mostly it'd
be the girls but my brother Gregory was awfully good at
flittin' us! He'd get my father's barrow and Lipton's tea box,
he'd put that on it and he used to flit us. If we fell out with
our sister he would come and flit us! He was very good, the
soul, he was a good brother, he was. But most of the time
he'd be needed in the croft anyway for something—except
when we flitted! And so, if you fell out wi' your sister, and
you weren't allowed in the larder you'd have to flit. You
could go to the pig house if there was no pigs in it—that
would be in the summer, but no' in the winter. When they
were empty we used to clean them and wallpaper them—
that's right! We used to paper them with leftover wallpaper,
and for paste only flour and water. You see, they were made
with railway sleepers and that would stick very well.

Then we'd pick plants for a kind of make-believe food.
We had the daisies—the big daisies were the fried eggs. The
brown docken seeds, that was mince and we had the leaves
of the docken for bacon, for the bacon and egg. We always
had a little vase of flowers, and we used to ask our mother
to come to visit us, and she was good fun. She used to come,
and she'd pretend she was drinkin' the tea out of one of
those beautiful bits of china and our make-believe teapot.
Oh everything was all make-believe, just anything we could
find. And we had a nice neighbour who lived quite near
us, was well to do, and she used to throw out some good

things. One day she threw out a clock, left it for us—she *left* if for us, she put it aside, and we loved that clock. Oh, it didn't work but it didnae matter. It didnae matter, it was a clock! You could turn the hands and put it on the shelf in the pig-house—oh we had good fun with that. And we used to go up the burn in the summer, and have nice wee houses up by the burn, just like the *aighridh* [sheiling].

We didn't need to buy things in those days—we could play for hours.

5

Not Always Peace and Quiet

The Suffragettes

Selina, Jean, Forbes, and Eliza
Comrie 1999

What about Aberuchill Castle, there was a fire there. It was burned down by suffragettes ... 1914, they did three mansion houses. One in St Fillans and The House of Ross and Aberuchill Castle... And we forget that nowadays you can get fire engines from all over to come. They only had horse drawn fire engines—one, only one. And who was going to get attention first? House of Ross was burned to the ground, but it was just a big tree outside Aberuchill Castle that was set on fire—it didn't do much harm. There was a big fire escape... Betty Comrie was in the castle at the time—there were three housemaids in there. There was a spiral stone staircase. It was just the big tree outside that went on fire so they were OK, but they got fire escapes after that— chutes that you have to go down, take off your shoes with heels—they're still there. That same night they were all set alight... the suffragettes all come from London, I expect. It was very odd, and awful to think that there were people in the house too when they set fire to it. And they had the cheek to make tea too, didn't they!

THE SCOTSMAN, 5 February 1914

SERVANTS' NARROW ESCAPE

The first discovery was made at Aberuchill Castle, where the only occupants were five domestic servants One of them awakened about 4.30 and discovered that her bedroom was full of smoke. She at once roused the other four servants, and they all with difficulty made their way downstairs, where the drawing-room furniture was seen to be ablaze, having apparently been saturated with paraffin or some other inflammable liquid. The castle belongs to Mr. G.C.L. Dewhurst, and is usually occupied by his mother (Mrs. Jones) but that lady had lately been residing with her mother at Craggish, Comrie. The servants at once proceeded to the estate offices about fifty yards away, and roused the workmen who lost no time in getting the castle fire appliances put into action. With an abundant supply of water to aid them, the men succeeded in confining the fire to the drawing-room, and there were greatly aided in their effort by … the fact that the wall between the drawing-room and the main part of the castle, being the original outer wall of the building, is three feet thick.

OLD PAINTINGS DESTROYED

All the furniture and furnishings in the drawing-room were destroyed, including a new grand piano and a number of valuable old paintings as well as the furnishings in several of the bedrooms above, where the servants had been sleeping.

The situation and the white walls of the castle make it a conspicuous landmark from the railway and the highway between Comrie and St Fillans. It dates back to the year 1602, but was added to in 1869 and 1874. It was in one of the added wings that the fire was discovered.

A quantity of suffragette literature was found lying about the place, and also an empty oil can, which smelt of paraffin. The damage will amount to several hundred pounds.

THE SCOTSMAN, **5 February 1914**
HOUSE OF ROSS — DAMAGE BETWEEN £3000 AND £4000

While some people from Comrie and the surrounding district were hurrying to the Aberuchill fire, two of them — a Comrie gardener and his son — noticed smoke issuing from the House of Ross. This house belongs to Mrs. Maclagan, but was wholly unoccupied, as the household are at present resident at Eton Terrace, Edinburgh. To this place Comrie Fire Brigade turned out when the alarm was given, but the firemen were powerless because of the lack of water. Here, again, apparently paraffin had been used, and to such effect that the fire blazed furiously, especially in the upper part of the building. Nothing could be done except to remove as much of the furniture as possible from the lower flat. This was done and the furniture was stored in the stable and coach-house.

LITERATURE AND A HAMMER

Here, also, printed suffragette literature was found lying about, and a small hammer, such as would probably be used for breaking windows, was found in the policies. Entrance had presumably been obtained by a staircase window so narrow, which was found open, though was left closed by the caretaker when he locked up the house on the previous night. The fire had evidently been started in a room above the main staircase, and it blazed in the building throughout yesterday forenoon.

The house, which was situated on rising ground adjoining the Comrie and Lochearnhead Railway, was built in 1908. The loss, it is computed, will amount to between £3000 and £4000.

About the same time people in St Fillans district, five miles further west, were attracted by a similar outbreak, which was discovered about 6 a.m. when Mr. M. Nicholson, a farmer at Artrostan, on the south side of Loch Earn, noticed flames issuing from the westmost house in the vicinity of the village — a two-storey villa, belonging to Mr. G. Stirling Boyd, an Edinburgh gentlemen, who resides there in the summer season. Mrs Stirling Boyd was chairman of the Edinburgh branch of the Anti-Suffrage

League...

This house, which was substantially built, and was also reduced to the bare walls, consisted of 3 public rooms, 8 bedrooms, a large hall, and other accommodation.

A WARM WELCOME TO LLOYD GEORGE

A sheet of notepaper had been carefully placed in a conspicuous part of the grounds, bearing the words— 'A warm welcome to Lloyd George.' There was also a suffragette booklet, dedicated in legible handwriting 'To Lloyd George.'

When the farmer noticed the outbreak he sent his daughter to St Fillans to inform Mr Stirling Boyd's gardener, but he and others who went to his assistance were powerless to check the progress of the flames. Crieff Fire Brigade arrived on the scene, but by that time the roof had collapsed and all the furniture had been destroyed, including the valuable paintings and presentation plate.

The house, which was built in 1904, was named 'Allt-an-fhionn' which is Gaelic for 'The Murmuring Burn'... Only the walls of the house remain, and the damage is estimated at over £3000.

POLICE INQUIRIES

Detectives from Perth assisted the police of the district in making inquiries into the occurrences yesterday. There is a local testimony that four ladies arrived at St Fillans by the midday train on Tuesday[49] and that two of them proceeded west through the village, while the other two went in the opposite direction towards Comrie; and later in the day two were seen at an old bridge in the neighbourhood of Aberuchill Castle, a most unusual place for visitors at this time of year.

---

49   Among them was Ethel Moorhead (1869—1955) who was convicted of arson and imprisoned in Carlton Jail in Edinburgh where she became the first suffragette in Scotland to undergo 'force-feeding'. (This involved a rubber tube being inserted into the throat or nose and liquidised food poured in via a funnel.) Perth prison was, however, the destination for many of the suffragettes and whose long campaign held newspaper headlines until after the First World War.

Selina, Jean and Eliza
Comrie 1999

They did it to get their vote (in 1918[50]), but we have no idea why they chose to do that, because they weren't political families.

Or were they?[51]

WARS AND RUMOURS OF WARS

And ye shall hear of wars and rumours of wars: see that ye be not troubled: for all these things must come to pass, but the end is not yet…

The Bible, Matthew 24:6

Dylan Fotheringham, age 8
Chapelhill, near Errol, 2010

My Grandad told me all about my great-grandfather who joined the Black Watch on the 23rd of July 1919. He served in Britain till 8th March 1920, then Germany from 9th March 1920 till July 13th 1922; in Britain from 14th July 1922 till 20th September 1937; in Palestine from 21st September 1937 till January 24th 1938.

He returned to Britain 25th January 1938 till 7th February 1938. He re-enlisted on 16th May 1940 as you can see from his documents (which have all been kept). He served in Scotland and was at the Liberation of Norway. The citation for the Liberation of Norway is signed by the King of

---

50 HOUSE OF LORDS—Thursday, January 10, 1918: REFORM BILL: WOMEN'S VOTE PASSED… Summarised, the *Representation of the People Act* granted the vote to women over 30 who were also householders, the wives of householders, owners of property worth over £5 or university graduates. The Act also granted the vote to all men over the age of 21.

51 The Anti-Suffrage League, the organization opposed to women having the vote, had a branch in Crieff, the vice-chairman of which was Mrs Stirling Boyd of 'Allt-an-Fhionn'.

Norway, which his family are very proud of as no other
Black Watch Soldier has one.

Rachel Brown, age 8
Errol, 2010

When my Granddad was a little boy in the 1930s he often
visited his granny who would be my great-great-granny.
She had six sons who all fought in World War I. Three sons
were killed in that war and the other three survived and
came home. All of them were in the army apart from my
great-granddad who was in the Royal Flying Corps. When
the war was over soldiers brought home souvenirs from the
war. One of my granddad's uncles brought home a German
soldier's helmet and my granddad's granny used this as a
flowerpot which she had hanging outside her home. My
granddad says that although the flowers were lovely the
helmet was a reminder of his uncle's bravery during the war
on the battlefields of France.

Andrew Robertson, age 10
Errol, 2010

My Granny and Granddad told me that my granny was a
war nurse. She said to me it was a really hard job to be a
war nurse, you would have to be fully trained because you
wouldn't want something wrong to happen in an operation.
There were lots of war men hurt, she felt really sorry for
them. I felt really sad after hearing the story because all the
people risking their lives for us and now their life is coming
to an end. My granddad found a bomb-shell during the war
and he gave the bomb shell to me to remember him.

Joanne, age 8
Errol, 2010

When my gran was a little girl she lived in Glasgow. It was the end of the war. My gran's family went for the Easter weekend to visit Comrie. In Comrie there was a prisoner of war camp. When my gran and her mum and dad were walking along the pavement two German POWs were coming towards them. As they got near the Germans clicked their heels together and stepped off the pavement. My gran wondered why they did this and her dad told her the reason was because they knew that Germany was the defeated nation. Although that was about 65 years ago she never forgot that moment. My gran's name is Edna Fogg.

Selina MacFarlane, Jean and Eliza Hyndman
Comrie, 1999

Selina: There was a prisoner of war camp at Cultybraggan. You'd see the German prisoners coming off the train and they walked through the village.
Jean: They had to walk up the main street. Yes, it was terrifying. They were actually Nazis—they weren't just ordinary Germans. It was terrifying 'cause they were so arrogant—the Panzer Korps from North Africa. I was still in school, I was only thirteen when the War started, so I was still in school. They marched up the street... from the station, and they sang and they were as arrogant as ever.
Eliza: The Panzer Korps prisoners were walking down through the village—that was when we first heard Lili Marlene—in German of course. And it was later we heard it in English... Sing it! Oh, it goes:

Underneath the lantern, by the barracks gate,
Darling I remember the way we used to wait,
'Twas there that you whispered tenderly,
That you loved me, you'd always be

My Lili of the lamplight, my own Lili Marlene.
Order came for sailing, somewhere over there,
All confined to barracks was more than I could bear
I knew you'd were waiting on the street
I heard your feet, but could not meet
My Lili of the lamplight, my own Lili Marlene.

There was quite a lot of them, a big train load at a time.
Very frightening it was.

Selina: A big camp, one of the biggest camps. There was
a little old lady grabbed me by arm one day as they were
coming marching down — they were so terribly arrogant.
And it was local or Glasgow soldiers that were looking after
them. She clapped my arm and said 'Don't you think it's
wonderful, our little soldiers marching and keeping charge
of these great big Germans?' I thought it was hilarious! She
was quite impressed you know, that people who weren't
able to go on active service and they were roped in to
looking after these prisoners! [laughs] They were here quite
a while; they used to be employed.

Jean: Yes, well later on they were employed, once the war
was nearly over. They stayed on, and some got married.
And the attitude to the local girl going out with a German
prisoner? It was accepted. Well, it was maybe different, take
for example, Carl was, he seemed to be such a nice person —
he was — and he stayed on in Comrie.

Eliza Hyndman: You see, at the end of the day, they were
people, young boys of fourteen, you know, who were just
press-ganged into the German army and they became
prisoners and they didn't really want to be [caught up in
the war]. They'd been living on their farms, working away,
minding their own business.

Jean: Not involved in politics like ourselves.

Eliza: And they worked on farms and so on, round here.

Selina: They did quite a lot of labouring.

Jean: We had poles in the fields to keep German aircraft
from landing, in every kind of flattish field, to keep gliders

from landing.

Eliza: Some of the German prisoners were really quite friendly; a lot of them didn't want to go to war at all.

Selina: I met quite a few, they were always very pleasant.

Pat MacNab
Comrie, 2008

That prisoner of war camp on Cultybraggan, it was the Italians that come in first and they were there and they were out working with all the farms. But then came the Jerries, they were the very worst lot that came, the tough boys that were there and they were guarded all the time. Twenty-four hour guard on them all the time. They didn't go out working in the farms, no, not then. And they hanged a man there because he gave them away—the other ones would be bullied the whole time they were in there they had a life of hell in it, bullied by their own people, the Nazis... ye see, I was away the six years, but there's a lot of folk in the neighbourhood that remembered them arriving and everything else.

And some of these prisoners worked on Ancaster Estates—they made use of them. They got all the roads made up, four miles up where I used to live and it was just a track, a sheep track. So Lady Jane had them made by the prisoners and got the wood to cut the last trees for the gate, you'll see the gate going in on the Langside Road after ye pass the toll road end and it goes right along the glen and right out on the top to the wee hill and they used to have it for going out to the shooting. And the guards, to supervise them, they came from the camp. And so she told the guards what she wanted. And that was four mile up the Glen road the prisoners made. Aye.

Jean Hyndman

There was Home Guard, poor folk that worked all day in their ordinary work and then they had to go out after work and look after these prisoners in Cultybraggan.

Jimmy Stewart

Being an agricultural worker, in Balquhidder at the time, I was exempt so I was in the LDV in these days—that's the local volunteers, the Home Guard. [52] I finished up Sergeant there. We did training, mostly the shooting side of it and among the folk in the glen there were some good shots. We were used to a shooting anyway, being country folk. And there was a great man called Donald MacKillop, he was really a worthy, really! And the Commander-in-Chief was up one day when we were shootin' and he said, 'MacKillop!' he said (gruffly), 'How's your gun shooting?'

'Everything's well when it's held right, sir,' was his answer. He couldn't say very much to him efter that! (MacKillop knew how to hold a gun!)

Several planes come down though, quite near us—German planes. There was one particular one, who landed in strip of rocks in what they call Fans Glen, in Ballimore—they had another farm in these days called *Monachyle Tuarach* at the head of *Loch Voil*. One of the men always went up there in the winter time because there was cattle to feed there, and the sheep didnae come home until the night, and this day, this morning he went up, and it was grey and dark, and here this poor soul, a German airman, came towards him, with a broken leg. The LDV man took fright and he went straight back to Murlaggan and got a gun. And he said, 'If that bugger's got a gun I'll be sure to have one first!' But however, after he saw what had happened and what not, he took him in, and took him down to the main farm got him sorted oot there—he needed medical attention. And when he left hospital after the war was finished, that German pilot come back to see the people, and he said the best thing to ever happen was to crash the plane because he

---

52   The British Army defence organisation known as the LDV, Local Defence Volunteers, formed in 1940, changed its name to *Home Guard* to avoid the demoralising, satirical reference of 'Look-Duck-Vanish'.

could've been killed otherwise, if he'd kept on flying or if he'd landed anywhere else.

Christian Murray
Comrie, 2010

There were German prisoners of war sent over to work on the farm at Pitfour (Glencarse) and they were very good workers and very nice too. And when we spoke to them in German they were so pleased to have someone to talk to—their faces lit up when they heard we could speak their language. Well I don't suppose I could do it now but then—well at least we had learned enough to be able to talk to them. And one of them told us he had a family and children but he couldn't write to them, so we wrote letters for them and sent them and they were so pleased. They were hard workers and I think they stayed in one of the bothies. And I remember being surprised first because they were such nice people—I suppose because they were German and that was 'the enemy', I didn't expect them to be nice. But they really were. And I thought it was so sad that they had been sent so far from home.

Evacuees

Jean Hunter
St. Fillans, 2009

In 1939 when the War started our mother joined the ATS, although she actually joined it in 1938, I suppose as a Territorial or something. So the War came and she was involved with her ATS Work. My brother had left school— that's Charlie's father, he had left school and was working in the Bank in Perth. He was 17, anyway he was there, and Dad was still soliciting for his work as a Solicitor in Perth.

So they got a housekeeper and Nancy and I were sent to Crieff to stay with this Aunt and her; she had two sons, one was in the Scots Guards, he was in the army and the other was still at school. And three other cousins plus their Mother; another sister of my mother's, they came up to escape from the south of England, because they lived in Kent, up to Crieff. And we all descended on poor Aunt Mamie in her house in Crieff. Although her husband was there too, because he was a retired Army Officer, he was there. You know, she was landed with the six of us, you know, young, teenagers. Well she did. Her other sister was there too. So there was this household—suddenly, from just having her own family! Anyway we started school in Morrison's. Nancy was there for two years and I was there for seven, till I finished my schooling. I stayed with them six years then the last year they thought they had enough of me staying so I travelled from Perth daily, which was nice—I enjoyed that.

Eliza and Jean Hynman
Comrie, 2001

> **Eliza:** I was an evacuee. Well, I went to teach in Glasgow when I finished training, and they sent me, they evacuated me, everybody was evacuated, believe it or not to Glenlednock. Also during the war this house, Drumearn House, was used for evacuees .
> **Jean:** Oh yes it was a school.

LUMBERJILLS

Mary Mathieson
Lochearnhead, 2010

> During the War, I joined the Women's Timber Core, in Strathyre. I was just in my early twenties and there was a sawmill in Strathyre, and in 1941, I volunteered when my brother Donald said, 'They're lookin' for girls to work in the sawmill.' And I thought that that would be nice, so I went

and I got the job. And then after that, other girls came—
they were recruited when WTC was formed in 1942. My
other two sisters came and joined, and girls round about
here—we were the lumberjills. We had a uniform—airtex
shirt, kind o' browny shirt, a pullover, green pullover, and
a green tie, but that's your dress uniform. And we wore
britches, not for work, but for the dress uniform. And we
wore wool stockings up to the knees, and we're supplied
with very heavy brown shoes—over heavy! And we wore a
beret, with a tree badge on it, like a wee photo o' a tree. But
for our work we just wore overalls, like men would—bib
overalls, dark, like denim, wi' a bib, that's what we wore.
Well in those days, up until then, girls never wore trousers,
no, not here! My mother was used to it, she had seen it in
Glasgow so she didn't bother. It was sensible too and we
had black heavy boots, just like men's boots. Very heavy,
strong boots and warm—the shoes were for dress. And we
wore nice overcoats for work too, brown, good strong, like
the kind my father had when he worked in the railway.
Good strong waterproof material, good, good stuff.[53]

There was about sixty people workin' in Strathyre. And
they stayed in wooden huts, lovely huts with bunks, maybe
five on each side of every room and there was a stove.
Not too big, just ten bunks in each, Sometimes we went as
orderlies, to help them out, to make their beds sometimes,
to see that they kept their place nice. The girls didnae live in
Strathyre at all, they lived up nigh Balquhidder—separate.

And at first me and my sisters, we lived at home you
see, and cycled back and forth every day—Glen Ogle to
Strathyre every day, nae bother! We had our own bikes—
they weren't provided—push-bikes, fixed wheel. They
were good anyway. You'd go on your bike and you'd get
down there to start in the summer at half-past seven in the

---

53   At the end of the War, unlike the troops who served in the
armed forces, the women in the WLA and the WTC had to give back
every item of government issue clothing and were not allowed to
keep anything, even as a memento to their wartime service.

morning! All the way down into Lochearnhead, along past Balquhidder, and then away into Strathyre—oh, it didn't take long, just a wee while—you got used to it. Oh, yes, even that steep brae! Your feet on the handlebars on the way down, oh no crash helmets, no, no! And start working, then home at night, cycle up it on the way home. Steep? No, we were used to it.

There were girls as well, from Glasgow, and they were posted round by Balquhidder. An awful lot of Glasgow girls were there, girls that had worked with the glove departments and the scarf departments. They knew nothing about wood or anything and they were great—they loved it, out of doors, in the woods, they loved it.

And we'd an awful nice family of tinkers with us. At first some girls who weren't used to the tinkers weren't sure—they wouldnae work with them, they thought they were gypsies. But no, no, we knew them from way up north Perthshire, the ones who used to come round, the tinsmiths, and they were a good *craic*, a good yarn with them. Nice folk, yes, that's the kind. And we kept in with the tinkers because they were best at makin' tea in the snow, or the rain. Oh it was good. And they were workin' with us. And they were very musical—it was them had the band and them that could play for the dances. There was one a MacDonald—the MacDonalds came from Blair Atholl and I was friends with, one they called Mairi. And the brother was called Willy, he was working in the camp. It was the two sisters and a brother and they were very nice. They had a hut in Strathyre, so they stayed in Strathyre and mostly they were just working with us and getting a wee wage like the rest o' us. Four pound a week—of course we had to pay our debts out of it,[54] we'd pay our mother one pound fifty (nowadays)—thirty bob. Thirty shillings a week to our mother.

The girls who stayed in camp had their food there and we took a piece with us. No plastic bags in those days—you'd take the piece just in a newspaper (laughter). And then just sit down and eat it outdoors. Mother'd give us a good breakfast and we took a piece—it was usually that stuff called 'spam'. Spam, cheese, and jam. That was variety! Oh, no, we didnae have a flask, then. And my mother would make scones and she made homemade soup for us to have when we got home. And we used to fill our bags with kindling, from the sawmill, 'cause it was rubbish anyway. Our wee piece bag would hold the kindling and that was a good help to give my mother next mornin' for the fire.

We were rinding and peeling the logs—spruce, larch, every kind o' wood. And we loaded the wood, 4 x 2s, not the rest of it, but the 4 x 2s, they were all peeled and we loaded them onto a lorry. Gibson had the garage then and Gibson's lorry was on hire, but not the driver. And we took the wood onto the lorry, and some of us went to Strathyre Station and we took them off, to load into the big wagons. And they went south—heavy work, so there would always be two of us to lift the logs, like a team, always by twos. Two to cut, and as they were coming down, two to put on the wagon. Gloves! No, no (Laughter). And many a sore hand we had—no gloves and plenty of skelfs. We just helped one another, just do what we could, with a needle, very often, to take them out. Sterilize it, oh, not then. And sometimes, if one of those skelfs got festered, you'd get the district nurse to come. She was from Iona, Nurse

---

54   An article by James Hendrie in the *Forestry Journal* (Dec. 2009) states that the wage for girls over 19 the wage was 46 shillings a week (£2.30) out of which they paid for food and accommodation, with an option to pay National Health Contributions so they could qualify for 'free' medical treatment and full pay if they were ill for a week or less. (If longer, it was enough to cover their board and lodgings.)

MacMillan, she was awfully nice, a Gaelic speaker as well, from Iona. She lived in Balquhidder and she had a bicycle — she wasn't the nurse only for the camp, oh no, she was the nurse for the whole district so she came by bicycle.

There were men volunteered too, but they were all called up eventually. And the men had different jobs to us. See, we werenae allowed to touch the saws, but the men did the sawing, and it was circular saws, and very dangerous. But we did the peelin'. We had peelers and we would peel the bark off — not the two-handle spoke-shave but it was just one hand. We had Newfoundlanders too. You see they're like the Scots, aren't they? But you know what their ambition was? To marry a Scots girl! (laughter) That was their ambition! And they like music too, much like ourselves aren't they?

And we used to be up to the dances. There was a boy played the accordion, one of the MacDonalds fae Blair Atholl, he played the button box melodeon, and the other girl too, she played the accordion, and the third one sang — she had black hair with a rose in her hair. It was nearly all square dances — the Lancers, jig-time. And we had the eightsome reel, and the quadrilles, the Duke of Perth, Dashing White Sergeant. Oh we had a good time — great fun! Every Friday night there was a dance. Never a Saturday night — the thing stopped in case it would go into Sunday. They wouldn't allow that — no, nothing on a Saturday night. But Friday, very often it was Strathyre or in the hall by Balquhidder. Oh, there was good ones in Balquhidder. Not where the hall is nowadays, oh no, not the new one now, near the church. The hall in our day was on the road up, as if you were making for MacNaughtans, the Braes you know. To the left, a big wooden one — it's not there today, it's down. And that's a good way down to the Braes. And we'd cycle between Strathyre and Balquhidder.

And you'd come home after work on a Friday night and get changed, and go back to Strathyre to the dance — that's twice we'd cycle it on a Friday. We'd be home, changed, and to bed for a couple hours, and away again. And then you'd come back and it'd be the small hours in the morning, and the cockerels would be crowing up Glen Ogle, they'd be up at three in the morning! Then a couple of hours sleep and up in the morning, away again, until twelve o'clock at midday on the Saturday, when you'd stop then, midday, twelve o'clock. Oh it was good company, oh yes, good company, all the boys and girls were really nice people, they really were.. Lots and lots and lots of people met there— that's where I met my husband, he was working in the timber until he was called up—he was in the Black Watch. And do you know what he was? Wait 'til I get the name now—he joined the Woodpeckers. There was a regiment called the Woodpeckers. And after the war was over he was still out in Germany—he was two years out, you know, that was to do with the wood, to get Germany back to its usual again. He was trained at the wood, so he was a Woodpecker, and they were needed out in Germany for two years after the war finished.

On our day off, with the money we'd left after we gave some to my mother, we'd go to Stirling and have a lovely day! We took the train from Lochearnhead Station. We very often just walked down from Glen Ogle, didnae take us long, then took the train up to Balquhidder. Change over. Now this is before Mr. Beeching spoiled it all. What a shame it was. It's dreadful without it—look at that busy road now, that heavy traffic could be up in the railway!

But then my sister and I, we were shifted up to Bridge of Orchy. Way up, we were shifted, and wait till I tell you, the deer used to come down to the huts, and rattle at the bins looking for leftover food. The deer was so hungry, they'd come down. That was a hard winter and Mary and I were in the bunkhouse. Well, it was all right in the summer time, but in winter, these huts get so cold when the fires go down. You'd have just a couple of blankets and it got very cold at night, so ye kept the fire going all the time—take turns getting up to put a log on. I loved the summers, the lovely flowers. But oh dear, the midgies were awful bad because we were in a much wetter place, in a muddy soft bit at Bridge of Orchy—swampy and full o' midgies. Oh, we had to get that citronella stuff, it was supplied from the government. The Canadians used that—it helped a bit and I was glad to get it, we were so bad with the midgies that some days we were called off, we couldnae carry on, they were so bad.

After a while Mary had to leave 'cause she got sore feet, she got stuff off the wood and it affected her feet. I don't know what it was, somethin' to do with the wood. Then I left around '44, after I got married—my husband was called up—he was in the Black Watch. So then my sister and I were back home with my mother and my mother was glad because she had all these animals to do and she still had my father working. So there I was, I started the wood in 1941— that's the way it went.

The Women's Timber Corp was disbanded in 1946. For over forty years, the women who served in the Timber Corp and the Women's Land Army were not represented at the annual Armistice Day Parades. In 2006 Forestry Commission Scotland commissioned a sculpture as a national memorial to the women of the WTC. Unveiled in 2007, it stands in the Queen Elizabeth Forest Park near Aberfoyle.

LIFE ON THE FRONT LINES

Dr Walter Yellowlees
Aberfeldy, 2009

The war was a great gap in one's life really, you couldn't plan anything because the ruling was that when you qualified in medicine, as I did in 1941, you must do at least six months in hospital before you joined the services. I was always keen to do medicine—I think it was probably my dear mother who encouraged me in that respect, but then the war came. After qualifying, I did six months at Stirling Royal Infirmary and then I went down to join the RAMC, The Royal Army Medical Corp. The officers' training for RAMC was in Leeds, Beckett's Park, an old teacher training school—that was where doctors, now RAMC officers, were drilled. We trained for three weeks there, learning to march, to salute and all the rest of it. And they had a pipe band there and in those days I was a piper—I had piped at school, at Merchiston, and I enjoyed it. So I sent for my bagpipes because they were going to have a special parade through the town with the pipe band leading and I got my pipes and that was great. There was one considerable snag, though— a couple of days before this march, we were all vaccinated for small pox and my left arm was swelling up—it had had a big reaction, and as the left arm squeezes the bag, it was extremely painful to try and keep the drones going! But do I love pipe bands.

Training in weaponry of any kind, or defence? Yes, we were taught to use our revolvers, I think that was all. I remember going with the company sometime when they were doing assaults, training to go with them just to see what went on, which was very interesting. I was with the 51st Highland division. I joined in North Africa, I was in a field ambulance unit when the two armies met, the first army from Algeria and Tunisia came through— we all met in Tunis, and it was a tremendous meeting of the two armies and I was delighted to hear a Scottish accent. I remember—this was in Sicily, and I was going around the company, seeing all was well, and there were two chaps in a slit trench, and when I came, and they saw me, one says, 'I hear there's a new medical officer, oh the new doctor?' And the other one (knowing I could hear him) says, 'Oh he's no' a right doctor, he's jist a horse doctor!' (Laughs) There was wonderful banter going between the officers and the men— they were always pulling each other's legs.

In Sicily we made quite a lot of ground going in and the Germans had set up quite an offensive by the second or third day. And I was with the field ambulance—that's the unit behind the front line. There's a field ambulance with every brigade and I was with 152 Brigade's field ambulance. And the brigade had bumped the Germans where they'd got defences up and there was a pretty fierce battle going on. And the Camerons—if I say it this way it's rather blunt, but their own medical officer and their own commanding officer got injured. I was told it was a mortar bomb that hit a branch of one of the orange trees as it was fired. So it exploded and the medical officer and the commanding officer were both wounded, not mortally but they came to. I was behind and I was told immediately, 'Get your equipment and go up and take his place, with the Camerons.' The commanding officer, who was in a little tent we had, with his leg all bandaged up, he shouted out at me, 'Oh doctor, watch out for snipers in the orange groves as you go!' (Laughs) I was sitting in an ambulance to get there, and how I was to look out for snipers I don't know, but we didn't encounter any.

In many ways it was a tremendous experience to see Sicily and North Africa and to emerge still able to live and learn and continue being a doctor. It's quite interesting, in the RAMC we were taught—and it's quite right—that in warfare, usually there are far more casualties from illness and epidemics than there are from wounding. And that certainly was the case in Sicily because there was an outbreak of malaria, mercifully when all the fighting was finishing, and jaundice, there was an awful outbreak. It was quite interesting epidemiologically because jaundice was far more prevalent amongst the officers than the other ranks. This is because the officers had their Mess and they were sharing dishes and things, whereas the troops had their own little can, that was all, and so there was no mixing of utensils. It was very obvious among the officers that this was the case. Jaundice is caused by a virus—it's passed on from contamination, quite often from excrement. And in Sicily I managed to get a microscope—I didn't know that malaria was part of the population in Sicily but a lot of the chaps went down and it was very interesting doing blood smears and seeing the actual malarial parasite—it was wonderful! We were supposed to be protected by taking tablets of Mepacrine it was called but I think, perhaps, a lot of them weren't very strict in taking of their Mepacrine tablets. It was suppose to be a protector but we had a lot of cases of malaria. I remember our Padre, a wonderful chap, Coatie Smith, my last picture of him … lying in a slit trench shivering with a bout of malaria—awful.

Then in Sicily, at the end, when the fighting was over, we were static there, so the drill in the morning was: PT for the other ranks and for the officers—country dancing! (laughs) The Pipe major would take them, yes he did—I remember him teaching me how to dance a foursome reel. The Cameron Highlanders was a kilted regiment, but not in Sicily, not in battle—no, they kept their kilts out of the way until we got static.

After Sicily we were told that 'you're not going on to Italy— the 51st Division, Montgomery said he wants them for the invasion of Europe, for the second front— so you are going home for the winter,' which we did. In 1943, that was when we got home. I'm not sure it was a good idea that, because you got home … you got back in to all your relatives and family and then you've got to prepare for the next one—which was Normandy.

I was with the Cameron Highlanders by this time, I was the regimental medical officer of the 5th battalion and we duly got ready for the cross channel invasion—Normandy. And we got down the Thames, in quite a big boat, and then had to scramble down to landing crafts, we'd got (up the?) beaches and our Commanding Officer, who was Sandy Munro, he was a great chap, said, 'Where's the piper? Get him on the landing! The Camerons are coming back we must have a piper on the prow!' But poor bloke, the boat ran aground on a sand-bank and it came to a shuddering halt about a hundred or more yards from the beach and most of the chaps took their clothes off and waded through— things never go as you want them to go. But he piped, yes, he piped our way across.

We were lucky because—well, we were told this, that for the cross channel we were not doing an assault—it was Sword Beach we landed on and the battle had gone inland for a bit—we crossed Pegasus Bridge, which was one thing, we had to keep it from the Germans coming, because it was a key crossing of the Caen Canal. When we disembarked, after sailing from Sicily, we got home to Greenock

When I came out of the army and was demobbed I wanted to do several hospital jobs before I went into general practice— I had decided I wanted to be GP—at first got several residential hospital jobs and the last one I did was in Perth Royal Infirmary. One attraction of a job there was that my Uncle, John Primrose, had been Provost of Perth—we had visited quite often his Gannochy Farm just outside Perth and there was a bit of an attraction to go and work in Perth, which I did. While I was at Perth Royal Infirmary I obviously got to know a lot of the GP practices and a consultant I worked with, he told me one day that the senior partner in Aberfeldy was retiring and they were looking for a replacement. Perhaps these things are meant— and I've been here over sixty years.

Alastair Kissack
Dunira, 2008

Born in 1917, during the First World War, Alastair, like generations of his family before him, had a military career, which began after he left school and went to Sandhurst. He joined the King's Royal Regiment and during the Second World War he became lieutenant and temporary captain of the King's Royal Regiment. Remembered among the 'horse heroes', Alastair was heavily involved in the Normandy Invasion in 1944. Like many 'old soldiers' he spoke very little about it, was more inclined to talk of the bravery of others, making little of the fact that he was awarded the MBE in 1945: 'Oh, it was for the D-day thing...' When asked if he would tell his most memorable wartime story, Alastair had no hesitation in relating this story, which took him back to his school days in the 1920s:

Alastair: This was in the 1920s, at a school 'Speech Day', for boys who were twelve or thirteen—that was the Prep school—my brother Keith went there, he was four years older than me. And the school used to have a kind of open day for younger brothers—to see if they were suitable for the school, and to let them see what the school was like. And this was the Open Day, Speech Day—that's why I remember it so well. And this well-known war veteran came to talk to us—he had been decorated for his part in the First World War. And we were all sitting there, thinking this is going to be a wonderful story of blood and thunder in the trenches!

Well, on to the stage came this young man—and there was a blackboard behind him. And you could see that he had no arm, you could see from his jacket sleeve, only one eye, and crutches. And he got tremendous applause.... He got up, with great assistance he got up.

"When you go through life, you've only got to remember two words, and if you do, I guarantee you'll be happy when you die." And he turned to the blackboard and wrote:

'Be kind' and sat down.

It's quite true. But all the boys were most disappointed, you see. But looking back, it's a lovely story, and it's perfectly true. But the little boys were all disappointed because they thought it was going to be all blood and thunder and battle charges.

But it's just like I remember it—I won't forget. Be kind.

Lest we forget.

111

... 'Huntingtower', once the seat of Clan Ruthven, home to the Earl of Gowrie—he's the one who captured Mary Queen of Scots' son, James, and held him prisoner for a year (1582), then lost own his life over a second attempt. Huntingtower was forfeited to the Crown and then given to the Tullibardines.

6

PERTHSHIRE SONG

t comes to songs and song-makers, Perthshire is spoiled
ice on both counts. Some of the old ballads, which
bedded in local history and folklore, have long since
ck of their composers. Many of them have undergone
k process' that gives them their individuality, such as
gtower', once the seat of Clan Ruthven, home to the Earl
rie—he's the one who captured Mary Queen of Scots'
nes, and held him prisoner for a year (1582), then lost
life over a second attempt. Huntingtower was forfeited
Crown and then given to the Tullierbardanes. The castle
ks imposing and has a wealth of stories surrounding
s can tell you about the ghost of Lady Greensleeves,
mple, and she should know, as she lived near to the
gtower Castle for many years.

k House', home to the Oliphants of Gask, was, in its
ll known for its strong Jacobite ties, though perhaps
ryone who sings 'Bonnie Charlie's noo awa' knows
composer's father and grandfather could both speak
ersonal experience. On the march to Derby, Laurence
t was the prince's aide-de-camps and despite the
us battle of Culloden, their hopes and dreams were
ire several songs composed by the little girl who was
that house. Carolina Oliphant, later Baroness Nairne,
ontemporary of Burns and Scott, yet, in her day shied
om acknowledging that she had written so many songs.
her compositions and the popularity of her songs
d their own alongside Burns, Scott and Hogg, yet she
s comparatively little recognition. For this collection we

113

have selected only three of her songs, one of which, the much loved 'Rowan Tree', became the key to our earlier project in care homes. It was not simply an assumption that 'everybody knows it', but rather a revelation that the song itself had such a powerful effect on evoking memories, even among folk who had long since lapsed into silence.

It was these memories, which Doris and I recorded in 1999[1] that demonstrated to us the importance of song in keeping alive the cohesiveness that once characterised every community. Aside from her regular involvement with the Glenfarg Folk Club, Doris now hosts 'the House of Song' at the Celtic Connections Festival in Glasgow every January, which attracts a packed roomful of enthusiasts every night. The songs here are recorded on the CD by singers who have gathered there, or at one of our get-togethers, mostly at the 'Ochtertyre Song Weekends' and at one memorable weekend in Perth, Ontario. Two singers drove all the way from Quebec just to take part in a weekend of Perthshire songs. That surely speaks volumes for traditional song.

Scotland's finest song collector and song-maker of the twentieth century was a Perthshire man, Hamish Henderson (1919—2002). His love of Scottish tradition and his commitment to both Scots and Gaelic is reflected in the legacy he leaves, not only in the finest collection of songs, stories and traditions, but also in the inspiration that continues to fuel new collections.

---

1   Jean and Eliza Hyndman and Selina MacFarlane were recorded on those visits..

THE AULD HOOSE[2]
Carolina Oliphant (Lady Nairne), Gask, Perthshire

Oh the auld hoose, the auld hoose, what tho' the rooms were wee
Oh kind hearts were dwelling there, and bairnies fu' o' glee
The wild rose and the jesamine still hang upon the wa'
How mony cherish'd memories do they sweet flowers recall

Oh the auld laird, the auld laird, sae canty, kind and crouse
How mony did he welcome tae his ain wee dear auld hoose
And the leddy tae sae genty, there sheltered Scotland's heir
And clipt a lock wi' her ain hand frae his lang yellow hair

The mavis still doth sweetly sing, the bluebells sweetly blaw
The bonnie Earn's clear winding still, but the auld hoose is awa
The auld hoose, the auld hoose, deserted though you be
There ne'er can be a new hoose, will seem sae fair tae me.

Still flourishing the auld pear tree, the bairnies liked tae see
And oh how often did they speir, when ripe they a' wid be
The voices sweet, the wee bit feet aye rinnin' here and there
The merry shout o' whiles we greet, tae think we'll hear nae mair

For they are a' wide scatter'd noo, some tae the Indies gane
And ane alas! tae her lang hame, not here we'll meet again
The kirkyard, the kirkyard, wi' flowers o' every hue
Sheltered by the holly's shade, an' the dark sombre yew

The setting sun, the setting sun, how glorious it gaed down
The cloudy splendour raised our hearts, to cloudless skies aboon
The auld dial, the auld dial, it tauld how time did pass
The wintry winds hae dang it doon, now hid 'mang weeds and
   grass

---

2   Carolina Oliphant was born Gask House 1766 and though it was
demolished then re-built 1818 she was to remember it as 'home' till the
end of her life. Returning there as an old woman, by then in a feeble state
of health, one of her letters, griten two years before her death,

Gask, 25th November, 1843

Everything leads me back to early youth, and what has passed between my
first and last abode at Gask seems as a mixed and wonderful dream. Yet
mercy and truth have followed me all the days of my life.

THE LOCH TAY BOAT SONG[3]

Attributed to Harold Boulton

When I've done my work o' day
And I row my boat away
Down the waters of Loch Tay.
As the evening light is fading
And I look upon Ben Lawers
Where the after glory glows
And I think on two bright eyes
And the merry mouth below

She's my beauteous nighean ruadh
She's my joy and sorrow too
And although she is untrue
Well I cannot live without her
For my heart's a boat in tow
And I'd give the world to know
Why she means to let me go
As she sings ho-ree ho-ro

Nighean ruadh, your lovely hair
Has more glamour I declare
Than all the tresses rare
'Tween Killin and Aberfeldy
Be they lint white, brown or gold
Be they blacker than the sloe
They are no more worth to me
Than the melting flake of snow

Her eyes are like the gleam
Of the sunlight on the stream
And the songs the fairies sing
Seem like songs she sings at milking
But my heart is full of woe
For last night she bade me go
And my tears begin to flow
As she sings *ho-ree ho-ro*

---

3   *Queen Victoria, 1842*—Our row of 16 miles up *Loch Tay to Auchmore*, a cottage of Lord Breadalbane's, near the end of the lake, was the prettiest thing imaginable.... The boatmen sang two Gaelic boat-songs.

BUSK, BUSK BONNIE LASSIE [4]

Traditional

Dae ye see yon bonnie high hills, a' covered ower wi sna?
They hae pairted mony's a true love, an they'll suin pairt us
twa

Chorus
Busk Busk, bonnie lassie, aye an come awa wi' me
And I'll tak ye tae Glen Isla, near bonnie Glenshee

Dae ye see yon bonnie shepherd as he walks alang
Wi' his plaidie buckled roond him and his sheep grazin on

Dae ye see yon bonnie sodgers as they march alang
Wi' their muskets on their shooders an their broadswords
hingin' doon

Dae ye see yon bonnie high hills a' covered ower wi' snaw
They hae pairted mony's a true love, an they'll suin pairt us
twa

---

4 **Jimmy and Mary Stewart,** Crieff 2010
Jimmy: When Mary and I were first married we went way up Glen Isla, above Alyth. There was three shepherds in the place, a nice hirsel, nice sheep and everything, We were up there 1947, a terrible winter. We were cut off wi' snaw and planes dropping food to us…
Mary: But we were young—love's young dream!

HUNTINGTOWER[5]

Traditional

She:
When ye gang awa Jamie
Far across the sea laddie
When ye gang tae Germany
What will ye send the tae me laddie ?

He:
I'll send ye a braw new goon Jeannie.
I'll send ye a braw new goon lassie
And it shall be o' silk an gowd
Wi' valenciennes around lassie

She:
That's nae gift ava Jamie.
That's nae gift ava laddie
There's nae a goon in a' the toon
I'd like when you're awa laddie

He:
When I come back again Jeannie.
When I come back again lassie
I'll bring tae you a gallant gay.
Tae be your ain guid man lassie

She:
Be my guid man yersel' Jamie.
Be my guid man yersel' laddie
An tak me ower tae Germanie,
Wi you at hame tae dwell laddie

He:
I dinna ken how that wid dae Jeannie,
Dinna ken how that can be lassie
For I've a wife an bairnies three,
No shuir how you'd agree lassie

---

5   Other versions are known as 'The Duke of Atholl's Courtship' and 'The Duke o' Atholl's Nurse'. (See also notes to Child ballad 299)

She:
You should hae telt me that in time Jamie,
You should hae telt me that lang syne laddie
For had I kent o' your fause heart,
You'd ne'er hae gotten mine laddie

He:
Yer een were like a spell Jeannie
You een were like a spell lassie
That ilka day bewitched me sae
I couldnae help mysel lassie

She:
Gae back tae yer wife and hame Jeannie,
Gae back tae yer bairnies three laddie.
And I will pray they ne'er may thole
A broken heart like me laddie

He:
Dry that tearfu' e'e, Jeannie,
My story's a' a lee, lassie
I've neither wife nor bairnies three.
An I'll wed nane but thee, lassie

She:
Think weel for fear ye rue Jamie.
Think weel for fear ye rue laddie
For I hae neither gowd nor lands.
Tae be a match for you laddie

He:
Blair in Atholl's mine Jeannie.
Little Dunkeld is mine Jeannie
Saint Johnstoun's bower and Huntingtower.
An a' that's mine is thine lassie.

Duet:
Blair in Atholl's thine Jamie
Little Dunkeld is thine laddie
Saint Johnstoun's bower and Huntingtower.
An a' that's thine is mine laddie

QUEEN AMANG THE HEATHER
Traditional, as sung by Sheila Stewart[6]

Noo, as I roved out one summer's morn
Amang lofty hills and moorland mountain,
It was there I spied a lovely maid,
Whilst I with others was out a-hunting.

No shoes nor stockings did she wear;
Neither had she hat nor had she feather,
But her golden locks, aye, in ringlets rare
In the gentle breeze played around her shoulders.

"Oh," I said, "braw lassie, why roam your lane?
Why roam your lane amang the heather?"
For she says, "My faither's awa' fae hame
And I'm herding a' his yowes thegether."

"Noo," I said, "braw lassie, if you'll be mine
And care to lie on a bed o' feathers,
In silks and satin it's you will shine,
And you'll be my queen amang the heather."

"But," she said, "kind sir, your offer is good,
But I'm afraid it was meant for laughter,
For I know you are some rich squire's son
And that I'm a poor lame shepherd's dochter."

"But had you been a shepherd loon
A-herding yowes in the yonder valley,
Or had you been a plooman's son,
Wi' all my heart I would hae lo'ed ye."

Noo, I hae been to balls and I hae been to halls;
I have been in London and Balquhidder,
But the bonniest lassie that ever I did see
She was herding the yowes amang the heather.

So we baith sat doon upon the plain.
We sat awhile and we talked thegether,
And we left the yowes for to stray their lane,
Till I wooed my queen amang the heather.

6   Sheila's mother, Belle, used to sing the song and was often referred to as 'The Queen Amang the Heather'; this is also the title of Sheila's book about Belle.

THE SPRING O' TWENTY-EIGHT[7]
Composed by Duncan A. MacNab, 2002

When Tam Procter fell and broke his leg, his yowes were all in lamb
So he sent up tae Glen Artney tae hire me as his man
For Tam well kent that yowes in lamb just werenae goin' tae wait
And that's why I went tae Muirlanich in the spring o' twenty-eight

Noo the first eight miles I walkit, then I caught the baker's van
I piled inside amongst the bread, the broon, the plain, the pan
And he drappit me aff ootside Killin wi' a half-loaf and a cake
And I walkit oot tae Muirlanich in the spring o' twenty-eight

Chorus:
Where the hams hung frae the rafters, the swee was over the fire
The hens were in the kitchen and the coos were ben the byre
And the bonniest mare that ever ye saw was standin' by the gate
When I landed in at Muirlanich in the spring o' twenty-eight

Well I was just a laddie, only fifteen years o' age
But I could dae a day's hard graft for a pittance o' a wage
I'd lamb the yowes and twin the lambs from dawn richt through
   tae late
When I landed in at Muirlanich in the spring o' twenty-eight

Well my days were ayeways busy, my days were ayeways fu'
And how I loved tae work the mare when I hitched her tae the ploo
We blackit the haugh abla' the hoose and man those dreels were
   straight
When I landed in at Muirlanich in the spring o' twenty-eight

Chorus:
Where the hams hung frae the rafters, the swee was over the fire
The hens were in the kitchen and the coos were ben the byre
And the bonniest mare that ever ye saw was standin' by the gate
When I landed in at Muirlanich in the spring o' twenty-eight

---

7   A bothy-ballad composed by Duncan A. MacNab in the Spring
o' 2002 after visiting Muirlanich with his father, Pat MacNab. (Sung to the
tune *'If you've never been tae Kirrie'*)

Well I walkit up and doon the haugh and I fiddled and I bowed
The seeds they flew frae side tae side until they a' were sowed
And every nicht I'd groom the mare nae matter how I ached
When I landed in at Muirlanich in the spring o' twenty-eight

If ye felt the call o' nature there werenae ony loos
Ye just went ben intae the byre and squatted by the coos
But man, those days were happy and of that make no mistake
When I landed in at Muirlanich in the spring o' twenty-eight

Chorus:
Where the hams hung frae the rafters, the swee was over the fire
The hens were in the kitchen and the coos were ben the byre
And the bonniest mare that ever ye saw was standin' by the gate
When I landed in at Muirlanich in the spring o' twenty-eight

Well Tam Procter's leg it mendit, and the summer it had come
The crops they a' were plantit and the lambin' it was done
So a clappit the heid o' the bonnie mare as she stood there by the gate
And I bid fareweel tae Muirlanich and the spring o' twenty-eight

Chorus:
Where the hams hung frae the rafters, the swee was over the fire
The hens were in the kitchen and the coos were ben the byre
And the bonniest mare that ever ye saw was standin' by the gate
When I landed in at Muirlanich in the spring o' twenty-eight

THE ROWAN TREE
Carolina Oliphant (Lady Nairne)

Oh rowan tree, oh rowan tree, thou'lt aye be dear to me,
Entwined thou art wi' mony ties, o' hame and infancy.
Thy leaves were aye the first o' spring, thy flow'rs the simmer's pride
There wasna sic a bonnie tree, in all the country side.
Oh rowan tree.

How fair wert thou in simmer time, wi' all thy clusters white.
How rich and gay thy autumn dress, wi' berries red and bright
On thy fair stem were mony names which now nae mair I see.
But they're engraven on my heart, forgot they ne'er can be.
Oh rowan tree.

We sat aneath thy spreading shade, the bairnies roond thee ran
They pu'd thy bonnie berries red and necklaces they strang.
My mither, oh, I see her still, she smiled our sports tae see,
Wi' little Jeannie on her lap, and Jamie at her knee.
Oh rowan tree.

Oh, there arose my faither's prayer in holy evening's calm,
How sweet was then my mither's voice in the martyr's psalm
Now a' are gane we met nae mair aneath the rowan tree,
But hallowed thoughts aroond thee twine o' hame and infancy,
Oh rowan tree.

LUINNEAG
Le Seumas Stiùbhart, Maor-eaglais Bhlàir[8]

Air fonn—
Hò, mo Mhàiri laghach, 'S tu mo Mhàiri bhinn,
Hò, mo Mhàiri laghach, 'S tu mo Mhàiri ghrinn:
Hò, mo Mhàiri laghach, 'S tu mo Mhàiri bhinn
Mhairi bhoidheach lurach, Rugadh anns na glinn.

Nighean òg Dhiùc Atholl
Tha i tairis, ciùin;
Thug i spèis do'n Ghaidhlig
'S thug i gràdh do'n dùthaich

An ceann beagan laithean
Le mòr àgh is mùir
Bitheas i air a fàilteach'
Le Bàn-righ a chrùin.

Fhuair mi tiodhlac luachmhor
O'n òigh uasal choir;
Rinn i dhomhsa cràbhat
'Chumail blàth mo leòin.

Tha i tlusmhor, tlàth
'S i àluinn air gach dòigh,
'S air a figh' nas fhearr
Na dheanadh làmh Righ Deors'.

Be mo mhiann 's mo dhùrachd
Gum biodh Diùc aic' fhéin:
'S thigeadh beannachd dhùbailt
Air a dùthaich 's a linn.

I mar Bhan-righ Ester
'G iarraidh leas na tìr:
Is sheulaicheadh i fàbhor
Mar le fainn an Righ.

---

8   *Do Lady Evelyn Stewart Murray. Air dhi cràbhat a thoirt dha, a rinn in 'fhigheadh le a làmhan fhéin* (The Atholl Archive).

A Song
James Stewart, beadle of Blair Atholl Church[9]

The Duke of Atholl's young lass
She's compassionate and gentle
She appreciated Gaelic
And loved the home-land.

After a few days
With much suffering
She would be
With the crowned queen.

I got a precious gift
From the young noblewoman
She made me a cravat
To keep my frail self warm.

She is compassionate and gentle
Beautiful in every way,
Knitting me the very best
Fit for King George himself.

My earnest good wishes
To her own Duke
And may bounteous blessings
Be on them and their lineage.

She is like Queen Esther
Wishing the best for the land
And she sealed the favour
As with the King's own ring.

---

9   By James Stewart, beadle of Blair Atholl Church, to Lady Evelyn Stewart Murray, 1887. Who gave him a cravat, knitted by her very own hands. Lady Evelyn had heard that he was ill and she made this gift for him.

THE LAND O' THE LEAL[10]

Carolina Oliphant (Lady Nairne)

I'm wearin' awa', John
Like snaw-wreaths in thaw, John
I'm wearin' awa' to the land o' the leal.
There's nae sorrow there John
There's neither cauld nor care John
The day's aye fair
In the land o' the leal

Our bonnie bairnie's there, John.
She was baith guid and fair, John
And oh, we grudged her sair
To the land o the leal
But sorrow's s'all wear past John
And joys a-comin' fast, John
The joy that's aye to last
In the land o' the leal

Sae dear that joy was bought, John
Sae free the battle fought John
That sinfu' man e'er brought
To the land o' the leal
Oh dry your glistenin' ee', John
My soul langs to be free, John
And angels beckon me
Tae the land o' the leal

Oh! Haud ye leal and true, John
Your day is wearin' through, John
And I'll welcome you
To the land o' the leal.
Now fare-ye-weel, my ain John.
This warld's cares are vain, John.
We'll meet, and we'll be fain.
In the land O' the leal

---

10   The song is also known as 'I'm Wearin' Awa', John' and was
composed by Carolina Oliphant in 1798 for a close friend, Mrs Campbell
Colquhoun of Killermont, who was mourning the death of her first child.
Lady Nairne composed the song, set to a tune she loved and sent with a
letter of condolence to Mrs Colquhoun, hoping she would take comfort
in the thought that the little one had gone to a far better place, 'the land o
the leal.'

The Braes of Balquhidder
Poem by Robert Tannahill [11]

Will ye go, lassie, go, to the Braes o' Balquhidder
Where the blaeberries grow, 'mang the bonnie bloomin' heather;
Where the deer and the roe, lightly bounding together,
Sport the lang summer day 'mang the Braes o' Balquhidder

Chorus
Will ye go, lassie, go,
To the braes o' Balquhidder!
Where the blaeberries grow,
'Mang the bonnie bloomin' heather

I will twine thee a bower by the clear siller fountain
An' I'll cover it o'er wi' the flowers o' the mountain;
I will range through the wilds, an' the deep glens sae dreary.
An' return wi' their spoils tae the bower o' my dearie

When the rude wintry wind wildy raves roun' our dwellin',
An' the roar o' the linn on the night-breeze is swellin'
Sae merrily we'll sing as the storm rattles o'er us,
Till the dear sheiling ring wi' the light liltin' chorus.

Now the summer is in prime, wi' the flowers richly bloomin'
An' the wild mountain thyme a' the moorlands perfumin'
To our dear native scenes let us journey together
Where glad innocence reigns 'mang the Braes of Balquhidder

---

11   In 1958, the McPeake Family from Belfast released their record of
'Will Ye Go, Lassie Go' based on Tannahill's poem. Before long it had taken
off across the world, becoming better known than the poem that inspired
it. The Captain S. Fraser's *Collection of Melodies of the Highlands and Islands
of Scotland,* 1816, includes a melody, Bochuiddar—Balquhidder (No. 77)

The Lass of Glenshee[12]

Composed by Andrew Sharpe, c. 1805

One fine summer's morning as I went out walking
Just at the breaking of dawn o'er the sea
I happened to spy a fair, pretty damsel
Out tending her flocks on the hills of Glenshee.

Said I, 'Pretty fair one, if you'll be my dear one
I'll take you over, my bride for to be
And I'll dress you up in fine silks and satins
And likewise a footman to wait upon thee.

'Oh no, kindly sir, you will not take me over,
I don't want a footman to wait upon me
I would rather stay home in my own homespun clothing
And tend to my flocks on the hills of Glenshee.

Said I, 'Pretty fair one, you don't understand me,
I'd take you home my own bride you will be,
And this very night in my arms I will hold you.'
So she gave consent and she came on with me.

For twenty long years we've both been together
Seasons have changed but there's no change in me
And if God lets me live and I have my right senses
I'll never prove false to the lass of Glenshee.

She's Mary, my Mary, my own darling Mary
As sweet as perfume that blows over the sea
And her cheeks are as fair as the white rose of summer
You'll find in full bloom on the hills of Glenshee.

---

12   This song, which was published as a broadside ballad, became
very popular with farm workers all over rural Scotland (See Ord's *Bothy
Songs and Ballads*, pp 75−76). It also travelled the world and many versions turn up across the Atlantic such as this one, from Newfoundland.
(Laws O6, Memorial University of Newfoundland Folklore Archive)

THE LAIRD O' COCKPEN[13]
Carolina Oliphant, (Lady Nairne),

The laird o' Cockpen, he's proud an' he's great,
His mind is ta'en up wi' things o' the state;
He wanted a wife, his braw house to keep,
But favour wi' wooin' was fashious to seek.

Down by the dyke-side a lady did dwell,
At his table head he thought she'd look well,
McCleish's ae daughter o' Claversha' Lee,
A penniless lass wi' a lang pedigree.

His wig was weel pouther'd and as gude as new,
His waistcoat was white, his coat it was blue;
He put on a ring, a sword, and cock'd hat,
And wha could refuse the laird wi' a' that?

He took the grey mare, and rade cannily,
An' rapp'd at the yett o' Claversha' Lee;
"Gae tell Mistress Jean to come speedily ben,
She's wanted to speak to the Laird o' Cockpen."

Mistress Jean she was makin' the elderflower wine;
"An' what brings the laird at sic a like time?"
She put aff her apron, and on her silk gown,
Her mutch wi' red ribbons, and gaed awa' down.

An' when she cam' ben, he bowed fu' low,
An' what was his errand he soon let her know;
Amazed was the laird when the lady said "Na,"
And wi' a laigh curtsie she turned awa'.

Dumfounder'd was he, nae sigh did he gie,
He mounted his mare an rade cannily;
An' aften he thought, as he gaed through the glen,
She's daft to refuse the Laird o' Cockpen.

And now that the laird his exit had made,
Mistress Jean she reflected on what she had said;
"Oh, for ane I'll get better, it's waur I'll get ten,
I was daft to refuse the Laird o' Cockpen".

---

13   Tune, 'When she cam' ben she bobbit'

Next time that the laird and the lady was seen,
They were gaun arm-in-arm to the kirk on the green;
Now she sits in the ha' like a weel-tappit hen,
But as yet there's nae chickens appear'd at Cockpen.[14]

---

14   The last two verses, which give the song a happy ending, were
added by Miss Ferrier.

Will Ye No Come Back Again
Carolina Oliphant (Lady Nairne)

Bonnie Charlie's noo awa
Safely o'er the freendly main
Mony's a heart will brack in twa
Should he ne'er come back again

Chorus
Will ye no come back again
Will ye no come back again
Better lo'ed ye cannae be
Will ye no come back again ?

Ye trusted in your heilan' men
They trusted you, dear Charlie
They kent you'r hidin' in the glen
Death or exile braving

English bribes were a' in vain
Tho' puir and puirer, we maun be
Siller canna buy the heart
That beats aye for thine and thee

We watched thee in the gloamin' hour
We watched thee in the morning grey
Tho' thirty thousand pounds they gie
There is none that wad betray.

Sweet the laverock's note and lang
Liltin' wildly up the glen
But aye tae me he sings ae' sang
Will ye no come back again.

GRIOGAL CRIDHE[15]

Traditional

'S iomadh oidhche fhliuch is thioram,
Sìde nan seachd sian,
Gheibheadh Griogal dhomhsa creagan
Ris an gabhainn dìan.

> *Air fonn*—
> *Obhan, obhan, obhan iri*
> *Obhan iri o!*
> *Obhan, obhan, obhan iri*
> *'S mor mo mhulad, 's mor.*

Eudail mhoir de shluagh an domhain,
Dhoirt iad t' fhuil an dé
'S chuir iad do cheann air stob daraich
Tacan beag bho d'chre.

B' annsa bhiodh le Griogal Cridhe
Tearnadh chruidh le ghleann,
Na bhith Baron mòr na Dalach,
Sioda geal ma m'cheann.

Chaneil ubhlan idir agam
'S ubhlan uil' aig cach
'S ann tha m'ubhal curaidh caineil,
'S cùl a chinn ri lar.

Nuair bhios mnathan òga 'bhaile
Nochd 'nan cadal sèimh;
'S ann bhios mis' air bruaich do lice
Bualadh mo dha làimh.

---

15   Composed for Gregor MacGregor beheaded at Taymouth, c. 1574

Translation

Glen Lyon Lament
(Beloved Gregor)

Many a night, cold and wet
In every kind of weather
Griogal would find for me a rock
Under which I could shelter.

Chorus
O-van-o-van etc.
Great is my sorrow — great.

Dearest beloved of all the people on earth
They spilled your blood yesterday
They stuck your head on an oaken spike
Some distance from your body.

Better to be with Gregor of my Heart
Bringing cattle down the glen
Than to be with the Baron of Dull
With white silk about my head.

I have no apple at all[16]
When every one else has one;
My sweet fragrant apple
Lies with his head on the ground.

When the young wives of the village
Sleep peacefully tonight
I will be lying on your tomb
Beating my two hands in grief

16   the apple was an analogy for the highest compliment that could
be paid to a sweetheart.

THE FREEDOM COME-ALL–YE

Hamish Henderson[17]

Roch the wind in the clear day's dawin'
Blaws the cloods heelster gowdy ow'r the bay
But there's mair nor a roch wind blawin'
Through the great glen o' the warld the day
It's a thocht that will gar oor rottans
A' they rogues that gang gallus fresh an gay
Tak the road an' seek ither loanins
For their ill ploys tae sport an' play

Nae mair will the bonny callants
Mairch tae war, when oor braggarts crously craw
Nor wee weans fae pit- heid and clachan
Mourn the ships sailin' doon the Broomielaw
Broken faimlies in lands we've herriet
Will curse Scotland the brave nae mair, nae mair
Black an' white ane til ither mairriet
Mak' the vile barracks o' their maisters bare

So come a' ye at hame wi' freedom
Never heed whit the hoodies croak for doom
In your hoose a' the bairns o' Adam
Can find breid, barley bree an' painted room
When Maclean meets his freens in Springburn
A' the roses an' geans will turn tae bloom
And a black boy fae yont Nyanga
Dings the fell gallows o' the burghers doon.

---

17   Thanks to Kätzel Henderson for permission to include the song. For an account of Hamish's life, poetry and songs see: Timothy Neat's Hamish Henderson: *A Biography*, Vol. 1, *The Making of a Poet (1919—1953)* and Vol. 2, *Poetry Becomes People (1954-2002)*, Edinburgh (Polygon), 2007 and 2009. *Collected Poems and Songs* by Hamish Henderson, edited by Raymond Ross, Edinburgh (Curly Snake Publishing), 2000. See also the collection of essays, *Borne on the Carrying Stream—The Legacy of Hamish Henderson*, edited by E. (Paddy) Bort, Ochtertyre (Grace Note Publications), 2010.